T H E

PROBLEM

W I T H

WHEN FOCUSING ON YOU HOLDS YOU BACK

SELF

SIMON WARRINGTON

HELP

SELFISH
BOOKS

For skeptics

"Self-help books are the pornography of self-improvement. They offer the illusion of a quick fix and feed our insecurities, making us feel inadequate while promising a better life just out of reach."

Unknown

CONTENTS

CHAPTER 1
ME, MYSELF, AND I

A recurring theme in self-help is the idea that you're broken, or at least a little bit fucked up. Modern pressures like career demands, social media, relationships, and generational trauma are often blamed as the root causes. Then comes the pitch: you need fixing, and here's how if you just buy into this shiny new idea.

But are we being sold the lie that we're inherently flawed and in desperate need of a quick fix? Has self-help simply turned into yet another product we consume?

Maybe the real problem with self-help is right there in the name—it's all about the self. And that's the issue. You're so focused on yourself that you can't actually help yourself. What if the issue is that there isn't a problem to solve? What if life isn't a puzzle to assemble or a competition to win? What if it's about embracing the journey, with all its imperfections and uncertainties?

The self-help industry, a multi-billion-dollar powerhouse, has exploded in recent years, offering solutions to almost everything—from financial struggles and relationship woes to personal development and spiritual awakening. In the following chapters, we'll explore the history and commercialization of the self-help industry, dissect its promises and failures, and consider better alternatives. We'll look at the illusion of control perpetuated by many self-help books and how this leads to frustration and disillusionment. We'll examine the narcissistic tendencies fostered by self-help and the impact of comparison culture on mental health.

Most importantly, we will discover alternative paths to personal growth—paths emphasizing community, consciousness, and acceptance. These paths encourage us to embrace our imperfections and find meaning not only in our achievements but also in our connections. We'll cut through the noise of the self-help industry and uncover a more sustainable, fulfilling approach to true #wellness.

When I first picked up a self-help book, I was captivated by the promise of transformation. The cover promised a happier, more successful version of myself, and I eagerly dove in. Like many, I was searching for a way to improve my life, to find that elusive secret to happiness and success just out of reach. However, as I delved deeper into self-help, I found an unsettling truth: the more I focused on self-improvement, the more self-centered I became. This irony is central to the problem with self-help. And here's the kicker—while I'm looking to solve the problem of self-help, I'm acutely aware this publication is just another self-help book.

Self-help books sell hope, promising that with the right mindset, habits, and routines, you can achieve anything. The allure is powerful: it taps into our deepest desires for control, success, and happiness, convincing us that we're just one book, seminar, digital course, or motivational quote away from transforming our lives. But are these authors and gurus really just "hope dealers," administering a quick shot rather than offering lasting change? Their promises have merit. Many self-help principles, such as setting goals, practicing gratitude, and cultivating positivity, can be beneficial. However, problems arise when the pursuit of self-improvement becomes obsessive, leading to perpetual frustration and self-criticism.

We are entering a new era of mental health solutions, dominated by self-help gurus and their expensive online courses, all promising to enhance our mental performance. Meanwhile, social media floods us with brain-hack memes designed to keep us clicking and consuming motivational slop. All of this is playing out against the backdrop of a turbulent eco-political climate—Trump, war in Europe, soaring inflation, and alarming suicide rates among young men. It's no surprise that people are desperately seeking answers to the eternal question: *How can I be happy?*

Over the past decade, my journey into self-help and personal growth has spanned a wide range of experiences, teachings, and practices. I've explored Brené Brown's insights on vulnerability, the Dalai Lama's teachings on compassion, Eckhart Tolle's mindfulness practices, and Russell Brand's irreverent spirituality. Along the way, I've dived into Michael Singer's *The Untethered Soul* on consciousness, Robert Bly's *Iron John* on masculinity and mythology, and countless podcasts like Jeff Krasno's *Commune* on personal growth and social change and Nicole LePera's *Self-Healers Soundboard* on holistic psychology.

But my growth hasn't been limited to books and podcasts.

I've participated in traditional and experimental therapies, attended men's retreats for brotherhood and personal growth, and explored body-spirit alignment weekends. I've delved into the subconscious with hypnosis, completed the Landmark Forum, and embarked on solo travels through South America, Cambodia, and Vietnam. Those solo journeys, where I faced the challenges of navigating unfamiliar worlds alone, taught me more about myself than I ever learned from a book. Combined, these experiences have profoundly shaped my understanding of self-awareness, personal growth, and what it truly means to *be*.

I've come to realize that true fulfillment doesn't come from relentless self-improvement but from cultivating community and meaningful connections. While self-awareness and growth have their place, they need to be balanced with empathy, compassion, and a broader perspective—one that comes from understanding others and our role within the larger fabric of society. Self-help books and programs often push us to look inward, scrutinize every thought and behavior, set ambitious goals, and constantly strive for more. But I've come to realize that true contentment doesn't come from constant inward focus. Personal growth isn't just about improving yourself—it's about looking beyond yourself and making a positive impact on the world around you.

One night, it hit me: in my obsession with perfecting my life, I was completely missing out on living it. I had become so consumed with fixing my flaws that I'd lost sight of my strengths and the beauty of imperfection. Gratitude and contentment had been overshadowed by an endless chase for more—I wanted it all, and it was never going to be enough. This realization marked the beginning of my journey away from an unconscious life—one consumed by the pursuit of money, endless consumption, and constant competition. It set me on a path toward a more conscious existence, one rooted in purpose, connection and personal revelation. Self-help books became my initial gateway to deeper self-reflection and discovery, ultimately guiding me toward a more fulfilling approach to life—one I hope to share with you in this book.

I believe true happiness and peace come from traditional practices and ancient techniques, not a doctor's prescription. The answers lie within, accessible through time-tested methods, because true healing is an inside job—something you'll uncover as you read further.

In this book, we'll delve into the complexities and contradictions of the self-help industry, examining how the relentless pursuit of self-improvement can often lead to greater self-centeredness and unhappiness. More importantly, we'll explore alternatives that emphasize connection, awareness, and acceptance—values that are often overshadowed in the traditional quest for personal perfection. I'll share my insights and research into understanding what truly matters. Together, we'll explore the self-help industry—its promises and pitfalls—drawing on the authors I've read, the traditions I've studied, and the wacky ideas found online.

As we embark on this journey, let's challenge the conventional—and often expensive—self-help wisdom and open our minds to a more grounded, human approach. This book is about striking a better balance between self-improvement and self-acceptance, between striving for better and appreciating what already is. Above all, it's about resetting our priorities.

At its core, this journey stems from my search for an answer to one profound question: *How can I better understand my mind and is that who I am?* Welcome to *The Problem with Self-Help*.

CHAPTER 2

THE SELF-HELP INDUSTRIAL COMPLEX

The self-help industry has grown into a multi-billion-dollar global industry, catering to an ever-expanding audience hungry for guidance on how to live better, happier, and more successful lives. What began in the 19th century with themes of individual responsibility and self-reliance has evolved into a sprawling network of books, seminars, apps, online courses, retreats, and coaching programs. Its size is staggering, with annual revenues in the tens of billions, fueled by a cultural obsession with personal improvement and the promise of transformation.

The movement, as we know it, has deep historical roots. It began with Samuel Smiles' *Self-Help* (1859), which championed personal accountability and improvement. His famous phrase, "Heaven helps those who help themselves," laid the foundation for what would become the mantra of modern self-help: take responsibility, let go, and take action. Smiles' work was a response to the challenges of the Industrial Revolution, emphasizing moral character and personal development as essential ingredients for success in an evolving world.

In the early 20th century, the self-help movement evolved,

heavily influenced by the New Thought movement. Napoleon Hill's *Think and Grow Rich* (1937) introduced the idea that positive thinking and visualization could lead to success. This period saw self-help merge with the American Dream, promoting the belief that anyone could achieve success through mental discipline and positive affirmations. Hill's message was simple: believe in yourself, visualize success, and the universe will conspire to make it happen. This optimism resonated deeply with the American psyche.

The post-WWII era saw a surge in self-help literature as people sought to rebuild their lives. Dale Carnegie's *How to Win Friends and Influence People* (1936) gained traction, emphasizing interpersonal skills and emotional intelligence. Carnegie's advice on effective communication and relationships made his book a staple for personal and professional success. The 1950s and 1960s introduced pop psychology, with Dr. Norman Vincent Peale's *The Power of Positive Thinking* (1952) cementing the idea that optimism could transform lives. Peale's philosophy that a positive mental attitude could overcome any obstacle found fertile ground in post-war America, ready to embrace hope and renewal.

In the 1960s and 70s, the self-help movement embraced countercultural revolutions, expanding human consciousness and exploring spirituality. Timothy Leary's mantra, "Turn on, tune in, drop out," encouraged inner exploration through psychedelics, while Ram Dass's *Be Here Now* (1971) blended Eastern philosophy with personal transformation. These decades blurred the boundaries between self-help and spirituality.

The Human Potential Movement of this era emphasized

unlocking human potential through intensive self-exploration. The Esalen Institute, founded in 1962 in Big Sur, California, became a hub for this lifestyle, offering workshops on psychology, spirituality, yoga, and meditation. Deepak Chopra, a frequent Esalen teacher, highlighted how our thoughts and behaviors influence our lives: "The way you think, the way you behave, the way you eat, can influence your life."

Esalen, Omega Institute, and Kripalu Center became prominent centers for holistic wellness, promoting long-term personal growth rather than quick fixes. Esalen was known for its openness to new ideas and willingness to push conventional boundaries. Workshops covered Gestalt therapy, a revolutionary approach focused on helping people stay present and connect with their immediate feelings, alongside yoga and meditation, all set against Big Sur's serene coastal backdrop.

The tone of self-help has shifted over time. Early themes revolved around discipline, hard work, and individual accountability. Over the decades, the focus broadened to include interpersonal success, emotional intelligence, and overcoming fear. By the late 20th century, wellness and spirituality became central, with practices like meditation and visualization entering the mainstream. In today's world, self-help is a hybrid of motivational psychology, wellness culture, and entrepreneurial hustle. It promises not just success but fulfillment, balance, and meaning—often packaged as "quick fixes" for a distracted, overworked audience.

However, commercialization has profoundly shaped the industry. Self-help is now a multi-billion-dollar business, generating $38 billion in 2024. The market often blurs the line between genuine guidance and profit-driven motives. Louise Hay's publishing company, Hay House, epitomizes this mix of self-empowerment and commerce. Its success, however, underscores how self-help can function both as a tool for healing and as a vehicle for profit.

Looking ahead, the future of self-help seems poised to become even more personalized and digital, leveraging artificial intelligence, data analytics, and virtual platforms to tailor solutions to individuals. The industry's increasing commodification may deepen the divide between those who can afford access and those who cannot, raising critical questions about its role in perpetuating privilege. As society grapples with rising inequality and global uncertainty, self-help may face mounting pressure to evolve from a tool of individual optimization to one that also emphasizes community, social equity, and collective well-being.

The Self-Help Boom

The 1980s and 90s marked the mainstreaming of self-help. Motivational speakers like Tony Robbins rose to prominence with his rock-star stadium tours and *Awaken the Giant Within* (1991). Robbins' high-energy seminars and intense participation pushed attendees to break through their limits. While Wayne Dyer blended psychology and spirituality in *Your Erroneous Zones* (1980), emphasizing the power of thought and intention.

Entering the 21st century, new voices and approaches reshaped self-help. Brené Brown's *Daring Greatly* (2012) brought a scientific lens to vulnerability and shame, bridging academic psychology with mainstream self-help. Influential figures like Iyanla Vanzant, Lisa Nichols, and Jay Shetty have further evolved the industry. Vanzant's TV show, *Iyanla: Fix My Life*, offered relatable, hands-on guidance to help individuals address personal challenges and heal emotional wounds. Nichols' transformational coaching emphasizes actionable strategies for personal empowerment and financial success, often spotlighted in her dynamic workshops and speaking events. Shetty's engaging social media presence, rooted in storytelling and mindfulness practices, has brought self-help to millions, making it accessible to a younger, tech-savvy audience. Together, they highlight how self-help continues to adapt to modern platforms and diverse audiences.

Brené Brown's work on vulnerability and shame resilience has deeply resonated, carving out a sub-genre of self-help centered on cultivating self-awareness. Similarly, Steven Kotler's exploration of flow states appeals to those seeking peak performance. Adding another dimension, Alok Vaid-Menon, a prominent LGBTQ+ activist and author, addresses issues of identity and self-expression, providing guidance and inspiration to the LGBTQ+ community.

Building on these modern voices, others have brought unique perspectives and styles to self-help. Ken Honda's *Happy Money* bridges financial wisdom and emotional well-being, while Jen Sincero's *You Are a Badass* and Kyle Cease's *I Hope I Screw This Up* inject humor and authenticity into the field, making self-help more approachable and relatable for a broader audience. Similarly, Mark Manson's *The Subtle Art of Not Giving a Fck** offers an irreverent, no-nonsense approach, challenging traditional self-help tropes and emphasizing the importance of embracing limitations and uncomfortable truths.

Continuing the evolution of self-help into the modern era, brands like Gwyneth Paltrow's GOOP exemplify the industry's shift toward blending wellness, lifestyle, and spirituality—often with a hefty price tag. Critics argue that GOOP's profit-driven approach contrasts starkly with the more free-spirited ethos of self-help in the 1970s, attaching luxury and exclusivity to advice that was once accessible to a broader audience.

Beyond GOOP, platforms like Mindvalley offer pricey courses promising transformative growth, while The Landmark Forum, with its steep fees and high-pressure tactics, often feels more like a recruitment program than genuine self-help. Similarly, biohacking brands like Bulletproof sell costly supplements and gadgets under the guise of optimizing health and performance, merging self-improvement with luxury wellness. Even apps like Noom and companies pushing law-of-attraction products, such as *The Secret*, monetize self-help ideas with subscription models and overhyped claims of transformation.

These examples highlight how self-help has evolved into a lucrative, commercialized industry. What was once rooted in accessible, community-oriented principles has become a high-cost commodity, often prioritizing profit over genuine healing or self-improvement.

Show me the Money

Tony Robbins' empire, worth over $500 million, and Louise Hay's Hay House highlight the commercialization of self-help—a natural progression as businesses capitalize on demand, drawing people in and then encouraging more consumption. Digital platforms and high-priced seminars have only amplified the industry's profitability. As self-help evolves, its dual identity as both a business and a tool for personal growth will play a key role in shaping its future.

Expanding on the commercialization of self-help, the rise of coaching and personal development programs highlights the industry's immense profitability. Many people willingly spend thousands on life coaches and workshops, believing these services hold the key to unlocking their potential and achieving success. This demand has fueled a new wave of self-help entrepreneurs offering one-on-one coaching, mastermind groups, and intensive retreats—often at significant costs. The term 'life coach' has become nearly as ubiquitous as 'influencer,' highlighting its growing prevalence and the rise of self-help teaching as a popular career path.

Self-help apps have also become a lucrative market segment. Platforms like Headspace and Calm, which provide guided meditations and mindfulness practices, boast millions of users and have attracted substantial venture capital. These apps capitalize on the growing interest in mental health on-the-go, offering convenient solutions for busy lives.

The commercialization of self-help is not without its critics. Many argue that the industry capitalizes on insecurities, offering quick fixes that often fail to deliver lasting results. For example, high-priced seminars promising transformation often leave participants feeling temporarily inspired but with little meaningful, long-term change. The pursuit of profit frequently overshadows genuine efforts to help, flooding the market with products that prioritize sales over substance.

Much of what modern self-help markets as innovative is often just a rebranding of ancient wisdom—mindfulness practices, for instance, rooted in Buddhism, are now sold as tools for productivity and stress relief, stripped of their original spiritual depth. Later on, we'll delve into the role of practitioners and gurus as "hope dealers," offering quick hits and temporary fixes while amplifying personal issues that may not even need solving.

In today's landscape, anyone with the right marketing strategy—emphasizing relatability, leveraging social media, and building a strong personal brand—can carve out a niche in self-help. The industry's growth is driven by digital innovation, charismatic leaders, the cult of personality, and a population increasingly eager for quick solutions to personal and professional challenges. While commercialization raises valid concerns about authenticity and exploitation, it also highlights both our enduring desire for growth and our fears of inadequacy.

As the self-help landscape evolves, it should aim to integrate ancient teachings more thoughtfully with modern approaches to address the demands of a rapidly changing world. Self-improvement needs to be reimagined as a sustainable lifestyle—woven into daily life over time—rather than a quick fix or temporary solution for perceived short-term issues. Self-help theory is not just another life hack; it's a way of living.

Winners and Losers

The world of self-help is filled with stories of triumph and heartache, illustrating the industry's potential and pitfalls. Let's review some real-life examples of success and failure in self-help.

Oprah Winfrey, while not exclusively a self-help guru, has embraced and promoted self-help principles throughout her career. Her book club, television network, and magazine prominently feature self-help content. Overcoming poverty, abuse, and discrimination, Oprah rose to become one of the most influential women in the media world. Her empire and philanthropic efforts highlight how she has used her platform to spread messages of hope and empowerment.

J.K. Rowling's story is another testament to self-help principles. As a struggling single mother on welfare, Rowling credits her success to perseverance and a positive mindset. Despite numerous rejections, she persisted in her writing. Today, she is one of the world's richest authors. Rowling's resilience and faith in her vision underscore the self-help message that persistence can lead to extraordinary outcomes.

Tony Robbins exemplifies success in self-help. Raised in a chaotic household, Robbins used the principles he now teaches to transform his life. By age 20, he was promoting seminars for motivational speaker Jim Rohn. Robbins integrated Rohn's teachings into his own high-energy seminars, creating a global following. His journey from a troubled youth to a motivational titan highlights how self-help principles can overcome adversity. Robbins' seminars, like "Unleash the Power Within," push participants to confront their fears and unlock their potential.

Not all self-help journeys end in success. Elizabeth Holmes, founder of Theranos, serves as a cautionary tale. Influenced by self-help and motivational speaking, Holmes had ambitious visions for revolutionizing the medical industry. However, her reliance on grandiose promises and positive thinking couldn't overcome fundamental flaws in her technology. The collapse of Theranos, amid fraud accusations, illustrates that self-help principles must be grounded in reality and practical application.

Similarly, the book and film *The Secret* promoted the Law of Attraction, suggesting that positive thinking alone could manifest wealth, health, and happiness. While this concept inspired many, others faced disappointment and financial ruin. Followers who invested heavily based solely on positive thinking often found themselves disillusioned when reality didn't align with their expectations. This narrative underscores the importance of coupling positive thinking with actionable steps and realistic expectations. After all, it may very well be the lack of action that holds people back—faith without work is dead.

Some individuals become trapped in a cycle of self-help addiction, moving from one seminar to the next in search of their next motivational high, yet failing to create lasting change. These 'self-help junkies' often invest heavily in books, workshops, and courses, only to remain stuck in the same patterns because they lack actionable steps or avoid confronting deeper, underlying issues. True self-improvement goes beyond simply consuming content; it requires commitment, honest self-reflection, sustained effort, and, in many cases, the guidance of a trusted mentor.

Ultimately, self-help is a tool, and its effectiveness depends on how it is used. When applied wisely, it can build great things; when misapplied, it can cause harm. The stories of success and failure in the self-help world offer valuable insights into how we can use these principles to improve our lives.

The industry's evolution from motivational books to a

sprawling enterprise highlights its adaptability. However, it's important to acknowledge how marketing and branding have become central to its success, often overshadowing genuine guidance. The digital age has further accelerated self-help's growth as the internet democratized access to resources. Platforms like Tik Tok and YouTube allow gurus to reach global audiences like never before.

CHAPTER 3
THE MARKETING OF SELF-HELP

Self-help marketing thrives on exploiting insecurities, repackaging age-old wisdom as revolutionary breakthroughs, and convincing people they're just one overpriced course or book away from fixing their lives. It capitalizes on a single, powerful marketing message: with the right tools and guidance, anyone can transform their life. This promise resonates with millions worldwide, driving an insatiable demand for self-help products and services.

At its core, the industry taps into our deep-seated desire to maximize human potential. But in a marketplace saturated with similar ideas—often just recycled versions of the same principles—how do authors, gurus, and teachers differentiate their offerings and stand out?

The primary tactic is to leverage emotional appeal, creating a sense of connection with the audience. Marketers—something we all are to some degree—understand that emotions drive purchasing decisions, which is why authors and gurus center their messaging around themes of hope and transformation. A seminar might promise to unlock your "limitless potential," while a book might guarantee "the secret" to success and happiness. Carefully crafted language, such as "break through your barriers" or "live the life you deserve," encourages us to believe we can overcome challenges like low confidence or financial struggles and achieve our dreams.

This approach is exemplified by Gabby Bernstein's workshops, which promote spiritual guidance with phrases like "manifest the life you want," and Mel Robbins' *The 5 Second Rule*, which claims to help readers transform their lives with simple, actionable strategies. Similarly, Rachel Hollis' *Girl, Wash Your Face* uses relatable anecdotes to inspire readers to stop making excuses and pursue their goals. These programs and books effectively tap into the universal desire for change, blending emotional appeal with practical tools to promise a better, more fulfilling life.

Marketing 101

Leveraging human connection is a fundamental principle of marketing, to bridge the gap between the consumer and the brand or idea. Once individuals connect emotionally, they are more inclined to make a purchase.

The language used in self-help marketing is carefully crafted to resonate with its target audience. Buzzwords and jargon create a sense of authority and expertise. Terms like "Unleash the Inner Badass," "The Universe Has Your Back," and "Fuck Like A Goddess" are designed to attract and engage readers.

The cult of celebrity and influencer marketing plays a significant role too. Are we buying a book because it's a genuine manual for change, or are we subconsciously drawn to the look, sound, and vibe of the guru behind it? Purchasing a book or course often feels like gaining entry to the teacher's "friend group," a subtle approval of belonging. More than just consuming their material, we're often buying into the persona of the guru—and likely much more than the manual they wrote.

Self-help teachers also invest heavily in crafting their personal brands—how they look, what they wear, how they sound, and how they present themselves on stage. In many cases, it feels like they're more salespeople than teachers or gurus, blending charisma with carefully packaged promises of transformation. For some, it edges uncomfortably close to snake oil salesmanship, where the focus on image and marketing overshadows the actual substance of their teachings.

These teachers also engage in strategic mutual promotion, appearing on each other's Instagram Lives, posting glowing reviews of fellow gurus' books, or including one another in email promos or newsletters. However, there's often a fine line— they're conscious not to over-promote a competitor, ensuring their own brand remains front and center.

Celebrity and influencer endorsements are key in this ecosystem, lending instant credibility to a product or service simply by association. A single one-liner endorsement on a book cover, or even a name listed on the back, can massively sway potential buyers scanning shelves for validation. An endorsement from Reese Witherspoon's book club, for example, can catapult a self-help book to bestseller status almost overnight.

Then there's the tactical sales piece—the online store optimization and the art of funneling potential buyers from awareness to purchase. Authors and marketers employ a range of strategies on platforms like Amazon and Google, optimizing listings with targeted keywords, encouraging positive reviews, and using digital advertising to reach specific audiences. For instance, they might bid on keywords like "best self-help books" or "how to improve self-esteem" to ensure their book appears high in relevant search results. Tools like Google's list of most-searched terms help authors tailor book titles and content to match what potential readers are actively seeking. A quick search for "best self-help books" on Google, for example, led me straight to *Pivot Year* by Brianna Wiest, available on Amazon, showcasing how effective these tactics can be.

Authors often use strategic tactics to boost their book rankings and visibility. Rallying their loyal audience to leave positive reviews on launch day is a common approach, enhancing credibility and increasing the book's appeal to potential buyers. Sponsored search listings and investments in high-performing keywords also drive traffic to sales pages, keeping the title prominently displayed.

Another effective strategy involves ticketed live events that include a free copy of the book. This ensures that each attendee contributes to the book's sales, helping to boost its chart performance and increasing the likelihood of achieving bestseller status. Securing a spot on the New York Times bestseller list—a highly coveted achievement—typically requires selling between 5,000 and 10,000 copies in the first week, making these combined efforts essential for success.

A widely used tactic is creating urgency. FOMO is a powerful motivator, frequently used to push sales. Self-help marketers leverage limited-time offers, exclusive access to bonus content, and countdown timers to create a sense of immediacy. If you add a book to your online shopping cart and leave it there for a few days, you'll often be retargeted with a special offer discount for the same book. These psychological and marketing tricks are carefully designed to guide you toward making a purchase.

Remember, self-help teachers are master manipulators. By combining a deep understanding of human behavior with sophisticated marketing techniques, they have built a finely tuned machine designed to maximize financial reward.

A significant challenge arises when potential customers gain substantial insights from podcasts, interviews, and promotional features. While these approaches effectively build awareness, they can unintentionally reduce the urgency to purchase the book or course. When too much content is shared upfront, the perceived value of the product diminishes, leaving potential buyers feeling they've already absorbed the core ideas without needing to commit financially.

The solution lies in offering a product that acts as a detailed guide or manual, providing actionable, step-by-step instructions that cannot be fully grasped through promotional content alone. This approach ensures customers view the book or course as indispensable for engaging deeply with the concepts. Marie Kondo exemplifies this strategy: her promotional appearances and media content generated immense interest, but it became clear that to truly implement her methods, we needed her book to access the comprehensive step-by-step process for decluttering and organizing. By positioning the product as essential, authors can preserve its value and necessity while successfully monetizing their expertise.

Platforms like Facebook, Instagram, TikTok, and X give self-help gurus unprecedented access to global audiences, allowing them to share content, engage with followers, and promote their offerings with seamless purchase paths. Rachel Hollis has leveraged social media to build a following of 1.4 million by sharing motivational quotes, personal stories, and behind-the-scenes glimpses of her life. Her ability to authentically connect with her audience has been a key driver of her success.

In addition to social media, podcasts and YouTube channels have emerged as highly effective platforms for disseminating self-help content. Many experts host their own shows, using these mediums to share in-depth insights and advice while fostering personal connections with their audience. Lewis Howes's *The School of Greatness* podcast and Alain de Botton's *The School of Life* channel both provide valuable strategies for personal growth. On the other end of the spectrum, the monks at Empty Cloud Monastery in New Jersey host the *Monk Chat* channel, offering thought-provoking Dharma content that, notably, remains entirely free.

Providing free content is a common marketing strategy in the self-help industry, with sample e-books, newsletters, and blogs serving to attract potential customers and build an initial audience. This free content serves as a gateway, providing audiences with a preview of what they can expect while building trust and engagement. For instance, James Clear, author of *Atomic Habits*, uses his popular newsletter to share insights and guide readers toward his paid products and courses.

Many self-help authors leverage platforms like Substack to

distribute newsletters, offering sample pages before a paywall for more in-depth content. Notable examples include Alice Vincent, who promotes her newsletter *Savour*, focused on life's small joys; Gail Muller, a life coach who organizes female-only retreats to foster support and self-reflection; and Laura Pashby, who leads nature-focused writing workshops designed to dismantle self-doubt and boost confidence. These authors use Substack to offer valuable content and foster community engagement in the self-help and personal development spheres.

Overpromising through flashy marketing pitches, exaggerated ads, and sensational titles can often land self-help authors and gurus in hot water. A significant ethical concern in the self-help industry is its tendency to overpromise and underdeliver. Many products make bold claims about their effectiveness, offering quick fixes to complex, deeply rooted problems. When these promises fail to materialize, they leave consumers feeling disappointed and disillusioned.

Controversial figures like Kevin Trudeau, who was fined for making false weight-loss claims, highlight this issue. Similarly, books like *The Four-Hour Work Week* and *You Can Heal Your Life* have faced criticism for offering overly simplistic or unrealistic solutions, with the latter even accused of promoting ideas that could undermine conventional medicine. These examples underscore the ethical challenges in self-help, where the pursuit of sales and sensationalism often comes at the expense of substance and integrity.

The marketing behind self-help products often involves a balance between compelling messaging and realistic expectations. Transparent communication about the potential benefits and limitations of a product is essential for maintaining trust. However, the truth is often not as marketable as an enticing promise. Many self-help gurus focus on exploiting the insecurities of their audiences rather than empowering them.

This often involves leveraging negative emotions like shame and fear to drive sales. By emphasizing the consequences of inaction or making individuals feel inadequate, marketers create urgency and pressure to buy. For instance, financial self-help advisors like Ramit Sethi, with his *I Will Teach You To Be Rich*, highlight the financial losses that can result from delayed action. Similarly, *The Dave Ramsey Show* podcast discusses the severe consequences of debt, advocating for Ramsey's financial methods as a means to prevent financial ruin. Through these tactics, the focus shifts from genuine empowerment to cultivating fear-driven urgency, pushing individuals toward immediate purchases with the promise of avoiding potential disaster.

While these tactics can be effective in the short term, they may exacerbate feelings of inadequacy and low self-esteem, counteracting the goals of self-help. In an industry reliant on trust and personal growth, authenticity and transparency are crucial. Consumers are becoming increasingly discerning and can often detect insincerity or deception. Authenticity involves being genuine and honest, while transparency means providing accurate information about products and services. Brené Brown's work on vulnerability and authenticity has become influential in promoting this more genuine approach to self-help.

The Future is Authentic

Authenticity and transparency will remain crucial as consumers demand more genuine and honest interactions. Building trust and maintaining ethical standards will be essential for sustaining success in the self-help industry.

Importantly, the future of self-help lies not just in individual gurus marketing their products to isolated consumers but in fostering vibrant communities. This shift towards community-centered self-improvement emphasizes collaborative growth, where the power lies within groups and networks of people who support one another in their personal development journeys. These connections cannot simply be 'sold to'; they thrive on mutual encouragement, shared experiences, and a collective commitment to growth, moving away from the transactional nature of traditional self-help marketing. The industry's future will hinge on the ability to nurture these relationships and build a more inclusive and supportive environment for individuals to thrive together.

As we've seen, much of the effort by self-help gurus is focused on promotion, raising the question of whether this diminishes the value of their work. If the primary emphasis is on marketing rather than genuine guidance, should we be concerned about the authenticity of what they offer? While the commercial nature of self-help can lead to significant profits, it begs the question: shouldn't these gurus prioritize sharing their wisdom freely, helping others for the greater good rather than simply capitalizing on people's struggles?

This tension between profit and purpose in the self-help industry challenges us to consider the true motives behind these teachings and whether they genuinely aim to uplift individuals or primarily drive sales.

CHAPTER 4
SELF-HELP'S MIRROR PROBLEM

The self-help industry, with its enticing promises of personal transformation and empowerment, often leads us down a path of excessive self-focus by encouraging an endless inward gaze. While self-reflection is undeniably valuable for growth, the problem with self-help is that it often becomes, quite simply, just *more self.*

This inward preoccupation can have unintended consequences: an inflated sense of importance, a heightened ego, and a relentless craving for validation from others to feel worthy. These effects ripple outward, straining relationships and diminishing our ability to form meaningful connections.

At its core, self-help promotes the idea that you have the power to change your life. While this can be a deeply inspiring message, it often shifts the focus inward to an unhealthy degree, where self-improvement turns into self-obsession. Self-improvement isn't meant to be a hobby or a way of life—it's a tool for growth. But like anything, too much self-help can trap us in a cycle of overanalyzing, overthinking, and never feeling "good enough." The belief that you are the master of your universe, capable of controlling every aspect of your existence, risks adopting a self-centered mindset. Instead of seeing ourselves as part of a greater community, we may start to view personal growth and happiness as the ultimate goal—often at the expense of developing connection with others or gaining a sense of belonging. So, what's the antidote to this relentless pursuit of self-improvement?

It's surprisingly simple: get off your arse and engage with the world around you. Help others. Commit to acts of service. Shift your focus toward contributing to someone else's growth, not just your own. True self-improvement happens when we step outside of ourselves, embrace our role within a larger community, and rediscover the joy and meaning that come from connection and giving.

While the self-help industry offers valuable tools for personal growth, it's important to be mindful of the potential for fostering too much focus on oneself as a solution. By prioritizing self-improvement with a focus on relationships, community, and humility, we can achieve a more rounded and fulfilling sense of well-being.

Remember, true personal growth isn't just about bettering yourself; it's about enhancing your ability to contribute to the world around you. Keep the following in mind, and you'll begin to feel more connected—to yourself, to others, and to the world you inhabit.

Embrace Humility: Recognize that you are part of a larger community and that your personal growth is intertwined with the well-being of others. Practice humility by acknowledging your limitations and appreciating the contributions of others.

This perspective helps ground you and prevents you from becoming overly self-focused.

Prioritize Relationships: Make time for the people in your life. Nurture these connections by being present, listening attentively, and showing empathy. Personal growth should deepen your relationships, not distance you from others. Don't shy away from sharing something about yourself—it gives others a point of connection and strengthens your bond.

Recognize Gratitude: Shift your focus from what you lack to what you have. Gratitude can help you appreciate your journey and reveal the support and love you receive from others. The phrase "attitude of gratitude" often highlights how focusing on what you have rather than what you lack can improve your overall well-being.

Engage in Service: Find ways to give back to a community. Helping others can provide a sense of purpose and fulfillment that goes beyond personal achievements. Volunteering or supporting local charity can connect you with a different group and offer perspective on the impact you can make.

Limit Self-Reflection: While self-reflection is important, it's also essential to take action. Don't get stuck in too much analysis. Set realistic goals and take steps towards them, accepting that mistakes are part of the learning process. Strive for progress rather than perfection and recognize that growth often comes from taking imperfect action.

Self-help literature often emphasizes maximizing productivity, enhancing performance, and achieving peak success. While the pursuit of excellence is commendable, the relentless pressure to improve can lead to burnout and feelings of constant inadequacy. Rather than finding satisfaction in your achievements, you may become trapped in a cycle of self-criticism, chasing the next goal without taking the time to appreciate what you've already accomplished.

Excessive self-reflection can also result in analysis paralysis. In the quest to understand and better yourself, it's easy to become overly introspective, questioning every decision and action. This overthinking can lead to inaction, where the fear of making a wrong choice prevents you from making any choice at all. Ironically, the pursuit of self-awareness and perfection can become an obstacle to living a full and engaged life.

Furthermore, an overemphasis on self-improvement can strain relationships. When personal growth becomes the central focus, empathy for others may take a backseat. You might prioritize routines and goals over quality time with loved ones, leaving them feeling sidelined and fostering a sense of isolation. This self-centered approach can damage connections and diminish the support systems vital for well-being.

The constant drive for self-optimization can also create a competitive mindset, where success is measured against others. Instead of fostering collaboration and mutual support, this comparison culture can breed rivalry and jealousy. You might find it difficult to celebrate the achievements of others, feeling threatened or envious instead. This undermines relationships and stifles personal growth, turning self-help into a source of division rather than connection.

CHAPTER 5

SELF-HELP IS A FIRST WORLD PROBLEM

Self-improvement is often focused on the eradication of negative thinking, which, while beneficial in many ways, may also be seen as a luxury for those who have the time and resources to prioritize personal growth. In today's chaotic world, self-help has grown into a booming and arguably much-needed industry. This raises an important question: Is self-help a luxury reserved for affluent societies, a privilege for the few, or does it have a place in all cultures and contexts?

The current focus on self-improvement often feels out of reach for many, making it seem like a product of privilege rather than a universally accessible tool for growth. It also raises the question of whether self-help is truly about personal transformation or if it has become just another commodity in the capitalist marketplace, consumed only by those who can afford it.

Moreover, the idea of self-improvement as a priority is itself a reflection of societal evolution. It signals a society that has moved beyond basic survival needs. The notion that anyone can improve their life through self-help, while appealing, can also imply that those who struggle do so because they have not tried hard enough to help themselves—ignoring the broader social and economic barriers they face. And is self-help a universal need, or is it primarily relevant to more affluent societies?

The contrast becomes stark when we consider the lives of those in regions torn apart by war, conflict, and oppression—places like Ukraine, Gaza, North Korea, various parts of Asia and Africa. In these regions, survival is often the primary focus of daily life. Their focus isn't on achieving personal enlightenment or climbing the ladder of self-actualization but on protecting their families, securing basic necessities, and making it through each day. When bombs are falling and homes are being destroyed, the idea of "finding yourself" or "unlocking your full potential" may seem trivial, even absurd. In these environments, the focus shifts from self to survival. The chaos of war or living under a brutal dictator forces people to live in the moment, not as a spiritual practice, but as a necessity. Every decision, every action is about immediate survival, not long-term self-improvement. Perhaps this forced present-moment living holds some unexpected benefits. Could it offer a mental focus that those of us in more privileged settings lack?

These points raise an important question: Is self-help a first-world problem? In places where conflict rages and basic human rights are under constant threat, the pursuit of personal growth is likely far from the minds of those simply trying to survive. The concept of self-care, so prevalent in developed societies, may feel irrelevant or out of touch in regions where the primary concerns are finding food, shelter, and safety. Could it be that the very luxury of time and security allows for this introspection, which, in turn, fuels a sense of dissatisfaction and disconnection? However, it's important to note that the people in these underdeveloped regions don't seem to lack resilience, wisdom, or inner strength. The struggles they endure often require profound emotional and spiritual fortitude.

According to Maslow's hierarchy of needs, when basic survival needs are at the forefront, higher-order pursuits like self-actualization take a backseat. Yet, this focus on survival and community doesn't diminish their strength; it may, in fact, enhance it. Are they stronger for it? Some research suggests that communities in conflict zones often exhibit remarkable resilience and a sense of solidarity that can be difficult to find in more individualistic, self-focused consumerist societies like those in Europe or the U.S. They draw strength from their collective experiences and shared struggles, which can foster a profound sense of purpose and connection.

There are tales of U.S. Vietnam veterans who, after returning home from the jungle, expressed a longing for the simplicity of war—not because they miss the violence, but because, in the midst of chaos, they were always present in the moment. On the battlefield, the mind is entirely focused on the here and now, leaving little room for the overthinking and reflection that can plague us in our daily lives. They also experienced a sense of purpose and connection to the community of their patrol or squad that often isn't present in civilian life.

As we explore further, it's essential to consider whether the self-help movement is relevant or even existent in regions where survival is the primary concern. Does the idea of "self" hold the same meaning across cultures, or is it a concept that takes on different forms depending on one's circumstances and upbringing? For example, are people in Gaza reading Eckhart Tolle and realizing all they need to do is "Let Go"? Probably not. Their focus is likely on much more immediate concerns, with little time for the luxury of soul searching.

Self-help takes on different forms across cultural contexts. In some societies, it's less about personal advancement and more about enhancing communication, building trust, and fostering harmonious relationships. The focus shifts to how self-improvement strengthens one's role within a community and contributes to collective success. However, given the disparities in access to resources, it's vital to consider how we can make self-help more inclusive and less of a luxury. Tools and theories of self-help should be freely available, not reserved for those who can afford pricey books or seminars.

But there's a deeper question here: Could this emphasis on self-help actually be contributing to the problem? In our quest to address every perceived flaw, are we creating issues where there might not be any? It's possible that by constantly reflecting on and analyzing ourselves, we're feeding a cycle of dissatisfaction, always seeking to 'fix' something that may not need fixing in the first place.

So, how do different cultures approach the self and is it something to be nurtured, controlled, or even diminished? In that examination, we can better understand the role of self-help, in a world where not everyone has the freedom to focus on personal growth.

Let's explore how different cultures and religious beliefs approach the idea of the self and examine whether self-help is a luxury afforded by peace and prosperity, or if it has a place in every society, even those facing the harshest conditions. By looking at perspectives from both developing and historical contexts, we can begin to understand the global landscape of self-help and the varying ways that different societies and communities comprehend the concepts of self and ego. What do they rely on when a Deepak Chopra podcast isn't within reach?

I have focused on religions and ancient philosophies because they serve as cultural constants and universal touchpoints for understanding and evaluating societies across borders, eras, and global communities.

Self and Ancient Philosophy

Ancient Greek and Roman philosophers laid the foundation for much of Western thought, including ideas about the self. Their explorations of human nature, ethics, and the pursuit of knowledge continue to influence modern discussions on personal identity and self-understanding.

Socrates, one of the most influential figures in Western philosophy, placed a strong emphasis on self-knowledge. His famous maxim, "Know thyself," reflects his belief that understanding oneself is the starting point for living a moral and meaningful life. Socrates argued that true wisdom comes from recognizing one's ignorance and constantly questioning one's beliefs and motivations. He believed that the unexamined life is not worth living, as it lacks the depth and self-awareness necessary for true fulfillment.

Socrates' method of inquiry, known as the Socratic method, involved asking probing questions to help others discover truths about themselves and the world. Rather than providing answers, he encouraged individuals to engage in critical self-reflection. This process of self-examination was seen as essential for achieving moral integrity and self-improvement. For Socrates, the self was not an isolated entity but deeply connected to ethical behavior and the pursuit of the good life.

Plato, a student of Socrates, expanded on his teacher's ideas and introduced the concept of the tripartite soul in his work *The Republic*. According to Plato, the self is composed of three parts: the rational, the spirited, and the appetitive. For Plato, a balanced and harmonious self is one in which the rational part governs the spirited and appetitive parts. This harmony leads to a just and virtuous life, where the individual's actions align with their true nature and the greater good.

Aristotle, a student of Plato, offered a more practical and human-centered approach to the self. He viewed the self as a rational agent, capable of making choices and acting in accordance with reason. Aristotle's concept of *eudaimonia*, often translated as "flourishing" or "happiness," is central to his understanding of the self. He argued that the highest good for humans is to live a life of rational activity in accordance with virtue. Aristotle believed that the self achieves fulfillment by cultivating virtues—qualities such as courage, temperance, and wisdom—through habitual practice. Unlike Plato, who emphasized the division of the soul, Aristotle focused on the unity of the self as a rational being that seeks to achieve its full potential through moral and intellectual development. For Aristotle, the self is not static but dynamic, constantly growing and evolving through deliberate action. He introduced the concept of the "golden mean," the idea that virtue lies in finding the balance between excess and deficiency in one's actions and desires. This balance allows the self to thrive and contribute to the well-being of society.

The Stoic philosophers, including figures like Epictetus, Seneca, and Marcus Aurelius, offered a unique perspective on the self, emphasizing the importance of self-control and inner peace. The Stoics believed that the self is not defined by external circumstances but by how one responds to them. They argued that true freedom and tranquility come from mastering one's emotions and desires, and from living in accordance with nature and reason. It truly is an inside job.

The Stoics taught that the self should focus on what is within its control—its thoughts, attitudes, and actions—while accepting what lies beyond its control, such as external events and the actions of others. This philosophy encourages detachment from material possessions and societal status, emphasizing instead the development of inner virtues like wisdom, courage, and justice.

Marcus Aurelius, a Roman emperor and Stoic philosopher, wrote in his *Meditations* about the importance of self-reflection and the discipline of the mind. He believed that the self should be guided by reason and should strive to live in harmony with the natural order of the universe. For the Stoics, the self is ultimately about cultivating inner resilience and maintaining a sense of calm in the face of life's challenges. Don't react to what's happening. Instead just observe it.

The concept of the self in ancient philosophy is rich and multifaceted, with each philosopher offering a different perspective on what it means to be human. From Socrates' call to "know thyself" to Plato's tripartite soul, Aristotle's focus on rational activity and virtue, and the Stoics' emphasis on inner peace, these ideas continue to influence contemporary discussions about identity, ethics, and personal growth.

These ancient thinkers laid the groundwork for understanding the self not just as an isolated entity, but as something deeply connected to reason, morals, and the broader community. Their teachings remind us that understanding ourselves and striving to improve are timeless pursuits, deeply connected to our search for wisdom and a fulfilling life.

The Buddhist View on Self

Buddhism offers a profound and often counterintuitive perspective on the concept of self, one that significantly diverges from the Western focus on self-improvement and individual identity. Central to Buddhist philosophy is the concept of *Anatta*, or "no-self," which suggests that the self as we commonly understand it—an independent, unchanging identity—is an illusion.

In Buddhism, the self is not seen as a fixed entity but as a collection of constantly changing physical and mental processes. This idea contrasts sharply with the Western self-help movement, which often emphasizes the development and enhancement of the individual self as a distinct and enduring identity. The Buddhist view challenges this notion by asserting that clinging to the idea of a permanent self leads to suffering. Instead, Buddhism encourages detachment from this illusory self and the recognition that our identities are fluid and interconnected with the world around us.

The practice of mindfulness, which has been widely adopted in the West as a tool for self-help and stress reduction, is deeply rooted in Buddhist teachings. However, in its original context, mindfulness is not merely about improving personal well-being or achieving a state of calm. It is a practice aimed at cultivating awareness of the impermanent and interdependent nature of all things, including the self. Through mindfulness, practitioners learn to observe their thoughts and emotions without attachment, ultimately realizing that the self is not a solid, independent entity but a dynamic process.

Buddhism also places significant emphasis on the eradication of ego, which is seen as the root of much human suffering. The ego, or the sense of a separate and autonomous self, creates a barrier between individuals and the true nature of reality. In contrast, much of Western self-help tends to focus on building up the self—enhancing self-esteem, setting personal goals, and achieving individual success. This focus on the self can be seen as reinforcing the very ego that Buddhism seeks to transcend.

The concept of *Anatta* directly challenges the self-help industry's focus on self-optimization. If there is no enduring self to improve, then the very foundation of self-help is called into question. Instead of striving to become a better version of oneself, Buddhism encourages the practice of letting go— releasing attachment to the self and the material world, and embracing the impermanence of all things.

However, this does not mean that Buddhism is entirely at odds with the idea of personal development. The teachings of the Buddha do offer a path to greater peace, wisdom, and compassion, but this path is not about self-improvement in the conventional sense. Rather, it is about awakening to the true nature of reality and recognizing the interconnectedness of all life. In this way, Buddhism offers an alternative to the self-help movement: a journey of inner transformation that goes beyond the self and seeks to alleviate suffering for all beings. For those exploring self-help within a Buddhist context, the goal is not self-optimization but the cultivation of mindfulness, compassion, and wisdom that transcends the self and sees us as a connected unit—we are all one.

The Christian View on Self

At this point, I think it's important to set the stage for what's to come and stay open to the idea of God—whether as an energy source, the universe, or simply a force beyond yourself. In the chapters ahead, we'll explore what divine practice can represent, whether as a form of faith, an act of surrender, or a perspective that helps us understand personal identity and communal responsibility. And don't worry, this isn't about becoming overly "God Squaddy." The focus remains firmly on the self and how we interpret it.

Christianity, particularly within the Catholic tradition, presents a view of the self that contrasts sharply with many aspects of the modern self-help movement. Central to Christian teachings is the belief that the self is not an end in itself but is oriented toward God and others. In this context, the self is understood as a creation of God, connected with a soul that carries ultimate significance. The focus is less on self-optimization and more on the cultivation of virtues such as humility, service, and love.

In Christianity, the self is fundamentally relational. The Bible teaches that humans are made in the image of God

(Genesis 1:27), and this divine imprint gives the self its inherent dignity and worth. However, the true fulfillment of the self is not found in pursuing personal ambitions or self-actualization but in living in accordance with God's will and serving others. The emphasis on serving others is a key point, highlighting that self-fulfillment in Christianity is deeply connected to the well-being of others.

The concept of humility is central to Christian teachings about the self. Rather than promoting the enhancement of the ego, Christianity encourages believers to humble themselves, to recognize their limitations, and to acknowledge their dependence on God. This humility is not about self-deprecation but about understanding one's place in the larger order of creation. It's about shifting the focus from self-centered concerns to a God-centered life, where the well-being of others takes precedence over personal gain.

Catholicism, in particular, places a strong emphasis on the soul as the core of human identity. The soul is seen as the eternal aspect of the self, destined for union with God. In this view, the ultimate goal of life is not to achieve worldly success or self-fulfillment but to prepare the soul for eternal life with God. This preparation involves a process of spiritual growth, often referred to as sanctification, which is achieved through prayer and acts of charity.

The Catholic Church teaches that the self should be directed toward the service of others, reflecting the teachings of Jesus, who emphasized love for one's neighbor as a fundamental commandment (Matthew 22:39). This focus on service is seen as a way to transcend the ego and align the self with God's purposes. In this framework, personal growth is not measured by material success or psychological well-being but by one's ability to live out the virtues of faith, hope, and love.

When viewed through a Christian lens, the self-help movement can appear somewhat at odds with traditional teachings. The emphasis on self-improvement, personal achievement, and self-esteem in much of modern self-help literature may seem to prioritize the ego over the soul. Christianity calls for a different approach—one that values humility over self-promotion, service over self-interest, and the soul's alignment with God over the pursuit of individual goals.

In this context, self-help becomes less about personal empowerment and more about spiritual transformation—about becoming the person God intended, not through self-will, but through grace. The goal is not self-sufficiency or independence, but a deeper reliance on God and a greater capacity to love and serve others.

While self-help in its secular form may prioritize personal achievement and self-optimization, the Christian approach calls for a reorientation of the self toward others, finding true fulfillment not in the self alone, but in a life lived in love and service.

The Jewish View on Self

Judaism offers a nuanced perspective on the self, balancing individual self-care with a strong sense of community responsibility. In Jewish teachings, the self is not just about personal development but also about how one's actions contribute to the betterment of the world. This perspective is deeply embedded in the concept of *Tikkun Olam*, or "repairing the world," which emphasizes the collective responsibility to improve society and help others.

The self is viewed through the lens of both individual and communal obligations. While self-care is important, it is never seen as an end in itself. Jewish teachings encourage individuals to take care of their physical and mental well-being, recognizing that a healthy self is better equipped to serve others and fulfill religious obligations. However, this self-care is always balanced with a sense of duty to the community and the world at large.

The Jewish tradition emphasizes that each person is created in the image of God (*B'tzelem Elohim*), which bestows inherent dignity and worth upon every individual. This belief underpins the importance of treating oneself and others with respect and compassion. The focus is not solely on the self but also on how one's actions impact the community and contribute to the greater good.

The concept of *Tikkun Olam* is central to Jewish thought and provides a framework for understanding the relationship between the self and the broader world. *Tikkun Olam* literally means "repairing the world," and it reflects the Jewish commitment to social justice, community service, and the pursuit of a just and compassionate society.

In this context, self-improvement is not just about personal fulfillment or individual success; it is about becoming a better person to contribute to the repair and improvement of the world. Jewish teachings encourage individuals to engage in acts of kindness, justice, and charity, not only as a way to improve themselves but also as a means of fulfilling their responsibility to others and to God.

Tikkun Olam underscores the idea that one's actions have a ripple effect on the community and the world. By improving oneself—whether through education, ethical behavior, or spiritual growth—an individual is better able to contribute to the collective effort of making the world a better place. This perspective aligns self-improvement with a broader mission, ensuring that personal growth is always linked to the well-being of others.

Jewish teachings on self-improvement are closely tied to the concept of *Mitzvot* (commandments). Observing the *Mitzvot* is seen as a way to refine one's character, deepen one's relationship with God, and contribute to the moral fabric of the community. Self-improvement in Judaism is therefore not just about personal satisfaction or success; it is about fulfilling one's obligations to society.

The practice of *Mussar* is a Jewish spiritual discipline focused on ethical and moral improvement. *Mussar* involves the study and practice of virtues such as humility, patience, and generosity, with the goal of cultivating a life of holiness and ethical integrity. This practice reflects the Jewish emphasis on self-improvement as a means of aligning oneself with divine will and contributing to the greater good.

Jewish teachings emphasize the importance of self-care, but this is always balanced with a strong sense of responsibility to others. As with the other religions we've explored, service to others is considered the path to follow—and perhaps the path out of your own head and problems.

The Muslim View on Self

Islam presents a distinct perspective on the self, where the concept of *Nafs*—often translated as the ego or self—plays a central role. In Islamic teachings, *Nafs* is viewed as a force within the human being that can lead one toward either righteousness or wrongdoing, depending on how it is controlled or purified. The Islamic approach to the self is deeply intertwined with the idea of submission to God (*Allah*) and the constant striving to align one's desires and actions with divine will.

In Islam, *Nafs* refers to the self, particularly in its aspect as the ego or inner desires that can lead one away from the path of righteousness. Islamic teachings identify different levels or states of *Nafs*, each representing a stage in the spiritual journey of a believer: *Nafs al-Ammarah* (The Commanding Self), *Nafs al-Lawwamah* (The Self-Reproaching Self), and *Nafs al-Mutma'innah* (The Tranquil Self).

The journey through each stage of *Nafs* is central to the Islamic concept of self-improvement. It involves a continuous process of self-purification, known as *Tazkiyah*, which includes practices such as prayer, fasting, service, and self-discipline. The goal is to purify the *Nafs*, bringing it into alignment with the teachings of Islam and achieving closeness to God.

The ultimate goal of the self is not self-actualization or personal achievement in the worldly sense but submission to the will of Spirit. The Arabic term "Islam" itself means "submission," and this concept is fundamental to the Islamic understanding of the self. A Muslim's life is centered around the belief that true peace and fulfillment come from surrendering one's ego and desires to God's will.

This submission involves recognizing that the self is not the master but a servant of God. The ego, or *Nafs*, must be controlled and refined through adherence to the teachings of the Quran and the Hadith (sayings and actions of the Prophet Muhammad). This process of self-purification is seen as essential for spiritual growth and for attaining a state of tranquility and contentment in this life and the hereafter.

Within an Islamic framework, self-help is interpreted through the lens of spiritual growth and moral development. The focus is not on self-optimization for personal gain but on refining the self in accordance with divine guidance. Islamic self-help emphasizes the importance of humility, patience, and perseverance.

Practices such as regular prayer (*Salah*), fasting during Ramadan, and giving charity (*Zakat*) are seen as ways to discipline the self and reduce the influence of the ego. These practices help Muslims develop qualities like empathy, gratitude, and self-control, which are valued not just for personal benefit but as acts of worship and faith.

The ultimate goal is not self-fulfillment in a worldly sense but submission to spirit and the attainment of tranquility through that submission.

The Hindu View on Self

In Hindu philosophy, the idea of self is layered. It revolves around two key concepts: Atman and Brahman. Atman is what we refer to as the individual soul or self, and it's considered eternal and divine. On the other hand, Brahman is the ultimate reality or the cosmic spirit that fills the universe.

What's really interesting is that, in Hindu thought, Atman and Brahman aren't seen as separate; instead, Atman is viewed as a part of this greater universal consciousness. The ultimate goal for many Hindus is to realize this connection, understanding that our true self (Atman) is actually one with the universal spirit (Brahman). This realization helps us break free from the cycle of birth and rebirth, known as samsara, and achieve liberation, or moksha. Practices like meditation, yoga, and self-inquiry play a big role in this journey, encouraging us to look within and grow spiritually.

So, the Hindu view of self really emphasizes the importance of self-awareness and our connection to the universe, helping us move beyond the ego and embrace something much bigger than ourselves.

The Cult View on Self

Cults and alternative religious movements often offer a distorted view of the self, focusing on the ego in ways that can be both alluring and destructive. These groups frequently manipulate concepts of self and ego to control their members, leading to psychological and emotional harm. Unlike mainstream religious teachings, which often emphasize humility, community, and the transcendence of the ego, these extreme belief systems tend to elevate the ego, often placing the leader or the group's ideology at the center of one's identity.

Aum Shinrikyo, a Japanese doomsday cult founded by Shoko Asahara, combined elements of Buddhism, Hinduism, and apocalyptic Christianity with the leader's own delusional beliefs. Asahara convinced his followers that the self must be destroyed to prepare for the coming apocalypse. The cult's teachings focused on the eradication of the ego, which Asahara claimed was the root of all evil. Members were subjected to extreme physical and mental conditioning to break down their sense of self, leading them to commit horrific acts, including the 1995 Tokyo subway sarin attack. The manipulation of the concept of the ego in Aum Shinrikyo illustrates how destructive beliefs about the self can lead to catastrophic outcomes, especially when divorced from the ethical and moral frameworks that guide mainstream spiritual practices.

Conversely, The Family, an Australian cult led by Anne Hamilton-Byrne, centered on the belief that its members were the reincarnations of highly evolved spiritual beings. Hamilton-Byrne convinced her followers that their egos needed to be completely subjugated to her will, as she claimed to be the messiah. The self was viewed as something to be molded and controlled entirely by Hamilton-Byrne, who used severe physical and psychological abuse to maintain control over her followers. The Family's teachings highlight the dangers of spiritual elitism and the idea that the self can be perfected only through absolute submission to a leader, contrasting sharply with mainstream teachings that encourage personal spiritual development and the ethical treatment of others.

These examples illustrate how the concept of the self and the ego can be twisted in extreme belief systems to serve the interests of cult leaders, fake deities, gods, or the group's ideology. Whether through the suppression of the ego, the destruction of personal identity, or the elevation of the self to cosmic significance, these movements often exploit the vulnerabilities of their followers by offering a distorted view of self-improvement or spiritual growth. And who's to say that mainstream religions aren't cults as well.

The Globalization of Self Help

The globalization of self-help has often resulted in cultural hybridization, where Western ideas blend with local traditions to create new forms of self-improvement. A notable example is the integration of mindfulness practices, rooted in Eastern religions like Buddhism and Hinduism, into Western self-help. While early Western self-help of the 1920s primarily emphasized individual responsibility and personal improvement, modern self-help has broadened to include wellness practices like meditation and chanting as tools for growth—perhaps taking on a more "woo woo" approach.

As mindfulness made its way to the West, it was reshaped to fit a secular and often capitalist framework, transforming into profitable products such as weekend retreats, online seminars, and trendy book titles. Ironically, these practices are now being re-imported to their countries of origin, but with a new focus on personal well-being rather than their original purpose of spiritual enlightenment.

The export of Western self-help ideas to non-Western cultures reveals a complex interplay between global and local values. As self-help continues to spread and evolve, it reflects the diverse ways people around the world understand the Self and its relationship to community, tradition, and the universe. However, these ideas are often accompanied by the individualistic ethos that defines much of Western self-help—emphasizing self-optimization, self-esteem, and personal success. In contrast, Eastern philosophies traditionally focus on connection—whether spiritual, communal, or personal—highlighting a significant difference in how these teachings are interpreted and applied. This contrast underscores the tension between Western ideals of "achieving more" and Eastern values of cultivating harmony and interconnectedness.

In countries like Japan, South Korea, and China, the idea of self-improvement is already deeply embedded in the culture, but it is traditionally linked to community harmony, duty, and the collective good rather than individual achievement.

In Japan, for instance, *kaizen*—the practice of continuous improvement—is a cultural norm that resonates with Western self-help's emphasis on personal growth. However, *kaizen* is often applied in a communal or corporate context. For example, in Japanese workplaces, employees might regularly engage in small, incremental improvements to their processes, not just for personal gain but for the overall success of the team or company. This contrasts with the Western focus on individual achievement, as in Japan, the improvement of the self is seen as a contribution to the success of the group rather than as an individual pursuit.

Similarly, in South Korea, the self-help industry has grown rapidly, but it often incorporates Confucian values, which emphasize family obligations, respect for authority, and social harmony. The Western idea of self-empowerment is often reinterpreted to align with these cultural values, emphasizing the role of the individual within the broader social structure rather than as an independent entity.

In China, where the concept of *guanxi* (networks or relationships) is central to social and professional life, self-help ideas are often adapted to focus on improving one's ability to navigate and strengthen these networks, rather than solely on personal advancement.

In other regions, such as the Middle East and Africa, Western self-help ideas have been met with more resistance, particularly when they conflict with deeply held traditional or cultural values. For example, the emphasis on self-empowerment and individual autonomy in Western self-help can be seen as contradictory to the importance of community and family.

In many parts of Africa, where community and kinship are central, the Western emphasis on individualism in self-help can feel out of place. Instead, self-help practices often prioritize collective well-being and the strengthening of communal ties. Traditional African values, such as Ubuntu—a philosophy centered on the interconnectedness of people—redirect the focus from individual achievement to the success of the community as a whole.

As we reflect on self-help's role in a world marked by deep inequalities, we must emphasize accessibility. Personal development shouldn't be an exclusive privilege—it should be a tool for empowerment available to everyone. This requires recognizing the unique challenges faced by different populations and creating resources that are relevant, culturally sensitive, and easy to access.

We must also acknowledge the ethical implications of promoting self-help in a world where many face systemic challenges. While personal growth is important, it cannot be a distraction from addressing larger structural issues such as poverty, lack of education, inadequate healthcare, and social injustice. Self-help should extend beyond the individual, aligning with a broader effort to uplift communities and create meaningful change. It should shift focus from "self" to "others."

As our world becomes increasingly interconnected, the self-help movement is poised for significant revolution. This raises an intriguing question: Will self-help remain a predominantly Western phenomenon, or will it adapt to meet the diverse needs of cultures and societies across the globe? With the rapid spread of ideas facilitated by globalization, and the rise of Gen Z and digital natives who are shaping the future with their modern views on gender, sexuality, work, immigration, and nationalism, the future of self-help may be more inclusive, diverse, and culturally sensitive than ever before.

The influence of Gen Z is particularly significant, as their approach to self-help goes beyond personal achievement or traditional markers of success. For them, it's about authenticity, mental well-being, and building a more inclusive world. Their approach to self-help is likely to prioritize mental well-being, social equity, and a rejection of rigid societal expectations.

Their engagement with global issues like immigration and nationalism may also drive the self-help movement to address themes of belonging, cultural identity, and cross-cultural understanding. As this generation navigates an increasingly globalized world, their influence could lead to a self-help movement that is more globally conscious, focused on collective growth, and aware of the social and political dynamics that shape individual experiences.

In many ways, self-help has been a product of Western consumer culture, where the focus on "self" and personal achievement aligns with broader societal values. However, as these concepts spread beyond their Western origins, they encounter diverse cultural landscapes where ideas about the self, community, and success differ greatly. This diffusion is beginning to reshape self-help itself, blending Western ideals with more communal perspectives. In some contexts, the emphasis is shifting from individual success to collective well-being, fostering approaches that prioritize harmony, interconnectedness, and shared growth over the pursuit of personal milestones.

Ensuring that self-help remains a tool for empowerment rather than a vehicle for cultural imperialism requires a commitment to inclusivity, cultural sensitivity, and ethical responsibility. This means creating self-help resources that are relevant and accessible to people from all walks of life, while also addressing the broader social and economic barriers that prevent access to them. It also means respecting the diverse cultural backgrounds of individuals and communities, ensuring that self-help content is not just a one-size-fits-all export from the West, but something that resonates with the unique experiences of people around the world.

In a truly online connected world, self-help has the potential to become a universal tool for personal and community growth, bridging cultural divides and fostering a more equitable approach to well-being.

Though often seen as a luxury for affluent societies, self-help has the potential to become a powerful tool for personal, community, and family growth across the globe. By making self-help more inclusive and accessible, we ensure that the pursuit of development isn't limited by economic or cultural barriers. Instead, it becomes a resource for building resilience and improving well-being for everyone.

When self-help prioritizes equity and collective well-being, it creates a more meaningful and sustainable path to personal and societal growth—for the greater good of all.

CHAPTER 6
THE ANTI-SELF-HELP MOVEMENT

The A-S-H movement critiques mainstream self-help, arguing that it prioritizes profit over genuine self-improvement. These self-help deniers reject its necessity, claiming it creates unrealistic expectations, commodifies personal growth, and fosters an unhealthy obsession with constant self-fixing. Critics warn that excessive self-reflection can lead to dissatisfaction and anxiety, suggesting it's sometimes better to simply live life rather than overanalyze it.

The industry's quick-fix promises often fall short. Critics stress that self-improvement is a lifelong process, not something that can be achieved through simple steps. This oversimplification diminishes the depth and complexity of personal growth.

Skeptics also highlight how self-help ignores external factors like social, economic, and political conditions, placing undue blame on individuals for circumstances beyond their control. Prominent voices like Barbara Ehrenreich, author of *Bright-Sided: How Positive Thinking Is Undermining America*, argue that the obsession with positivity often leads to denial of reality and neglect of systemic issues. While optimism has its place, she emphasizes the importance of confronting tangible challenges and seeking practical solutions.

One of the most notable figures who challenged the self-help industry's approach, is Mark Manson. If you've ever found the relentless pursuit of self-improvement to be more exhausting than beneficial, Manson's work is definitely worth exploring.

His bestseller, *The Subtle Art of Not Giving a Fuck*—notably successful in part due to its provocative title—serves as a manifesto for those seeking alternatives to the traditional self-help narrative that insists happiness is always a choice and that we should constantly chase it like a dog chasing its tail.

Manson touches on the illusion of constant happiness, and his approach is refreshingly blunt. He starts with a simple yet radical idea: Life sucks sometimes. No amount of positive thinking is going to change that. In fact, the more we chase after happiness as if it's some ultimate goal, the more miserable we end up feeling when we inevitably fall short. Traditional self-help books often peddle the idea that we can control our happiness by controlling our thoughts and actions. If only it were that easy! Manson calls out this illusion for what it is—an endless cycle of trying to fix ourselves, only to end up feeling more broken when we can't keep up with the self-imposed standards.

His solution is simple, but powerful: "Embrace the suck." He argues that it's okay to acknowledge that life is full of challenges, and instead of running away from them, we should face them head-on. This doesn't mean wallowing in misery, but rather accepting that difficulties are a part of life and that they don't need to be sugar-coated or avoided. Lean into it. This isn't really a new concept, but the way he frames it resonates with a new self-help audience—and it's more mainstream. Self-help shouldn't be complicated.

Take the idea of "not giving a fuck"—it's not about being indifferent or apathetic. It's about being selective with what you care about. We all have a limited number of fucks to give, so why waste them on things that don't matter? Instead of obsessing over being happy all the time, he suggests we focus on what's truly important to us, even if that means facing uncomfortable truths or dealing with hardships.

Another gem is his take on entitlement. Traditional self-help often feeds us the idea that we deserve happiness, success, and whatever else we set our minds to, simply because we're "special." Manson dismantles this notion with a reality check: We're not all that special. And that's okay! The belief that we are somehow entitled to a life free of pain and struggle is not only unrealistic but harmful. It sets us up for disappointment when life inevitably throws us curveballs.

By recognizing that we're not owed anything, we can start to appreciate the things we do have and focus on what we can control. This shift in mindset can be incredibly liberating. Instead of feeling let down when things don't go our way, we can learn to accept that suffering is a natural part of the human experience. More importantly, we can stop blaming ourselves when things go wrong, which is a trap that traditional self-help often sets for us.

Manson's approach is deeply rooted in the idea of values— what we choose to care about and prioritize in our lives. He argues that much of our discontent comes from having values that are out of whack. If we value things like success, fame, or being liked by everyone, we're setting ourselves up for failure because these are largely outside our control.

Instead, he suggests we focus on values that are within our control, such as honesty, integrity, or kindness. This makes so much sense.

Reframe Your Challenges

This shift in focus helps us reframe our challenges. Instead of seeing them as obstacles to our happiness, we can view them as opportunities to live out our values. For instance, if you value resilience, then a difficult situation becomes a chance to practice resilience, rather than just a source of frustration. This doesn't mean that hardships magically become easy to deal with, but it does give them a sense of purpose, which can make them more bearable. Our focus can shift to recognizing more than a need to control or suppress.

Another anti-self-help philosophy is the idea of letting go—specifically, letting go of the constant need to be happy. Borrowed from Buddhist teaching, this concept is simple and somewhat easy to apply. It doesn't mean giving up on happiness altogether, but rather understanding that happiness isn't something that can be forced or endlessly pursued.

This approach invites us to be present and fully engaged with our lives as they are, rather than striving for an idealized version of life that doesn't exist. It's about finding contentment in the here and now, instead of always chasing the next self-improvement milestone. After all, nothing truly exists outside the present moment—neither the past nor the future are real in the here and now. By letting go, we can release the pressure to constantly be better, do more, or achieve the next big thing.

This perspective represents a different kind of self-help—one that doesn't offer quick fixes or easy answers. Instead, it's about embracing the full range of human experiences, including the messy and uncomfortable parts. It's about recognizing that perfection isn't the goal and that it's okay not to have everything figured out.

In a world that constantly tells us to be more, do more, and have more, it's a reminder that we don't have to buy into the endless cycle of self-improvement and that it's okay to just be. We can stop giving a fuck about the things that don't matter and start focusing on what truly does. Life is messy, and that's what makes it beautiful.

Zero Fucks Given

Sarah Knight, author of *The Life-Changing Magic of Not Giving a Fuck*, has gained popularity by advocating for a more straightforward approach to life. Her philosophy centers on mental decluttering, prioritizing personal freedom over societal expectations, and rejecting the notion that everyone should follow the same path to peace of mind.

Like Marie Kondo's method of tidying up your home, Knight focuses on tidying up your mind. She encourages readers to take stock of everything they care about—whether it's their job, relationships, or even their social media presence—and decide what is truly worth their time and energy. This process of mental decluttering results in a life where you're no longer weighed down by societal pressures that don't serve you.

The idea of mental decluttering is incredibly liberating.

How often do we stress over things that, in the grand scheme of life, don't really matter? Knight gives us permission to stop giving a fuck about those things. Instead, she helps us focus on what truly matters, which is a radical departure from the traditional self-help message that often pushes perfectionism in every aspect of life.

One of the most refreshing aspects of Knight's philosophy is her strong rejection of societal expectations. Traditional self-help often implies that there's a "right" way to live, and if you're not on that path, you're failing. Knight flips this narrative by encouraging us to define our own path. She makes it clear that there's no one-size-fits-all solution for self-improvement.

Knight's message is particularly powerful for those who feel pressured to conform—whether it's getting married by a certain age, climbing the corporate ladder, or maintaining a perfectly curated Instagram feed. She reminds us that it's okay to opt out of these societal norms if they don't align with what we truly want. In her words, you don't have to give a fuck about what society says you should care about.

Her philosophy prioritizes happiness and well-being over the relentless pursuit of perfection, offering a refreshing contrast to traditional self-help narratives. Knight advocates for letting go of the guilt and anxiety that come from trying to meet other people's expectations. Instead, she promotes unapologetically making choices that serve your happiness and mental health, rather than trying to fit into a mold designed by others.

A cornerstone of Knight's work is the power of saying no. In a world where demands on our time and energy are constant, it's easy to feel obligated to say yes to everything to appear competent or kind. Knight challenges this mindset, encouraging guilt-free rejection of social obligations, work requests, or anything else that doesn't align with your priorities. By saying no to what doesn't matter, you create space to say yes to what does.

There's nothing overly complicated about Knight's message—it's straightforward and clear. In a culture that often tells us to do more, be more, and care more, Knight offers a refreshing counterpoint: care less about what doesn't matter and focus on what does. By prioritizing personal freedom over societal expectations, Knight offers a new approach to self-help—one that is simple, effective, and true to who we are.

The School of Life

I'm a massive fan of Alain de Botton. His *School of Life* channel on YouTube offers fantastic snippets of wisdom, and he's a speaker and author who brings a whole new perspective to the self-help conversation. If you're someone who finds typical self-help advice a bit too simplistic or feels like something is missing from the "do this, and you'll be happy" formula, then Alain de Botton is a name worth knowing.

The School of Life offers courses, books, and online content that encourage us to think deeply about our lives, our emotions, and our relationships—not in a way that promises immediate solutions, but in a way that fosters long-term growth and understanding. De Botton's approach is the opposite of the "quick fix" mentality that dominates much of the self-help industry. Instead of telling us how to be happy or successful in a few easy steps, he encourages us to engage with the world around us as the solution—to learn from the wisdom of the past, and to seek meaning in places we might not have thought to look—like a painting, a poem, or a philosophical text.

His work often revolves around the idea that wisdom and meaning are found through engagement with culture. He suggests that philosophy and art have the power to illuminate the complexities of human existence in ways that simplistic self-help books often overlook. Instead of offering step-by-step guides or bullet-point solutions, de Botton invites us to explore the rich tapestries of history, literature, and art as sources of comfort and understanding.

In his book *The Consolations of Philosophy* (2000), de Botton reintroduces us to the great philosophers of the past—think Socrates, Epicurus, and Nietzsche—who grappled with life's big questions long before "self-help" was even a thing. These thinkers didn't promise easy answers or a path to everlasting happiness, but they offered perspectives that can help us navigate the ups and downs of life with a bit more grace and understanding.

What makes de Botton's work stand out for me is his embrace of life's inherent complexity. Traditional self-help often tries to simplify our problems and offer straightforward solutions, but de Botton recognizes that life isn't always that simple. He understands that the human experience is messy and that sometimes, the best we can do is find solace in knowing that we're not alone in our struggles. His work seems to appreciate that life is not a linear experience and that it is filled with ups and downs, ins and outs.

He encourages us to find comfort in the nuances of life rather than trying to eliminate them. He invites us to see our challenges not as obstacles to be overcome, but as experiences that can deepen our understanding of ourselves and the world around us. It's a more holistic approach to self-improvement—one that doesn't shy away from the darker or more difficult aspects of life, but instead, sees them as integral to our growth.

This new kind of self-help is less about changing ourselves and more about enriching our intellectual and emotional lives—maybe thinking less and acting more. He reminds us that there's value in taking a step back from the hustle of self-improvement and instead, spending time with the ideas and works that have stood the test of time. Whether it's through reading philosophy, appreciating art, or simply reflecting on our experiences, de Botton shows us that there are many ways to find meaning and fulfillment that don't involve following the latest self-help fad.

This approach is particularly attractive for those of us who feel overwhelmed by the constant pressure to "fix" ourselves or solve every problem. De Botton suggests that maybe we don't need fixing at all—maybe we just need to understand ourselves better, engage more deeply with the world, and find beauty and wisdom in places we might not have considered before.

His work encourages us to slow down, think more deeply, and appreciate the richness of the human experience in all its layers. It's a reminder that sometimes, the answers we're looking for aren't in the latest self-help bestseller, but in the timeless ideas and works that have been guiding us for centuries.

Wisdom, comfort, and meaning are all around us if we're willing to look beyond the surface and embrace the enduring value of culture.

Acceptance of Uncertainty

The English writer and *Guardian* journalist Oliver Burkeman offers an honest take on the self-help industry's obsession with positivity—a perspective that, as a glass-half-empty person, I can resonate with. If you've ever felt like the relentless push to "think positive" is more tiring than empowering, then Burkeman's work is worth reading. His book, *The Antidote: Happiness for People Who Can't Stand Positive Thinking*, is exactly what it sounds like—a counter-narrative to the idea that we should always be striving for happiness through positivity.

Burkeman's approach is rooted in deep skepticism of the self-help industry's emphasis on positivity as the ultimate solution to life's challenges. He argues that the relentless pursuit of happiness through positive thinking can actually be counterproductive, leading to more anxiety and stress when life inevitably doesn't go as planned. Instead of constantly chasing after an elusive state of happiness, Burkeman suggests that we'd be better off accepting life's inherent uncertainties and embracing the full range of our emotions—including the negative ones.

This perspective is a radical departure from the typical self-help narrative that insists we can think our way to happiness. Life is full of struggles, and pretending otherwise does us more harm than good. One of the core ideas in Burkeman's work is the acceptance of uncertainty. Traditional self-help often encourages us to set goals, make plans, and take control of our lives to create a sense of certainty and predictability. But Burkeman points out that life is inherently unpredictable, and trying to control every aspect of it is not only impossible but also leads to frustration and disappointment. Instead of fighting against uncertainty, Burkeman encourages us to embrace it. This doesn't mean giving up on goals or ambitions, but rather recognizing that we can't always control the outcome—and that's okay.

Burkeman also argues that trying to eliminate negative emotions only makes them more powerful. His work explores how people from various cultures and philosophies have found peace by accepting their negative emotions rather than fighting against them. From Stoic philosophy to Buddhist teachings, Burkeman draws on a wide range of wisdom to show that accepting our emotions—both positive and negative—can lead to a more balanced and fulfilling life.

In a world that often insists on relentless positivity and control, Burkeman's philosophy is a welcome reminder that it's okay to not have all the answers, to feel uncertain, and to experience negative emotions. In fact, it's through accepting these aspects of life that we can find true peace and contentment.

Instead of endless introspection and constant self-improvement, these authors advocate for a more liberating approach—letting go of the need to control everything, stopping the overanalyzing, and embracing life as it is.

This perspective suggests that the answer isn't always found in more reflection or self-examination, but in accepting imperfection, focusing on what truly matters, and freeing ourselves from the pressure of relentless self-optimization. Less 'self,' more going with the flow.

CHAPTER 7
THE ILLUSION OF CONTROL

Within the self-help industry, a consistent theme is the promise of control. Many self-help books promote the idea that following specific rules or adopting particular mindsets enables individuals to master every facet of their lives, including destiny, emotions, success, and even the behavior of others. While this idea is appealing, it often leads to disappointment and stress, as it overlooks the inherent unpredictability of life.

The quote often attributed to Socrates, "The only thing I do know is that I know nothing at all," underscores the limitations of our understanding and the importance of acknowledging our ignorance. Recognizing that our knowledge is fundamentally incomplete liberates us from the unrealistic expectation of total control. This perspective encourages us to focus on what we can manage: our actions, attitudes, and responses. Embracing this awareness fosters personal growth, resilience, and a more compassionate approach to life. It encourages us to focus on what we can manage: our actions, attitudes, and responses.

For instance, self-help books with titles like *Mastering Your Destiny* by Thibaut Meurisse or *Total Control Over Your Life* by

Alan Lakein come with bold promises. Claims like "Unlock Your Full Potential in 30 Days" or "Achieve Unstoppable Success with These Five Steps" offer a sense of certainty and control that can be incredibly appealing. While aiming high is admirable, these promises often ignore the fundamental truth that some things are beyond our control. The idea that we can master every aspect of our lives through sheer willpower and the right techniques is alluring but fundamentally flawed. This misconception can lead us to believe that our failures are due to personal shortcomings rather than the complex mix of factors outside our control.

One major false promise is the idea that you can control your emotions. Books like *The Power of Positive Thinking* by Norman Vincent Peale suggest that with enough effort, you can banish negative emotions and maintain lasting happiness. However, emotions are complex and often unpredictable. While you can influence your mood and adopt a positive outlook, expecting to control your emotions completely is unrealistic. Emotions are not just fleeting experiences but deeply ingrained aspects of our psychological makeup, influenced by a myriad of factors including biology, personal history, and current circumstances.

Instead of trying to suppress our emotions, we should strive to understand and use them as tools. Emotions can provide valuable insights into our inner world and our needs. They are signals that can help us navigate life more effectively. Learning to manage emotions is different from controlling them outright. It involves acknowledging them, exploring their sources, and finding constructive ways to address them. This approach not only fosters emotional intelligence but also promotes a healthier relationship with ourselves.

Another big promise is that success hinges entirely on mindset and hard work. Books like *Think and Grow Rich* by Napoleon Hill and *The Secret* by Rhonda Byrne emphasize visualizing success and maintaining a positive attitude as keys to achievement. While mindset and effort are important, they are not the sole determinants. External variables such as economic conditions, social connections, luck, and timing significantly impact outcomes. Overlooking these factors can lead to unnecessary guilt and frustration when plans fail.

This illusion of success as purely a matter of mindset places undue emphasis on individual responsibility, ignoring systemic and structural challenges like economic inequality and discrimination. While determination and effort are valuable, they cannot always overcome such barriers. Recognizing this broader context helps set realistic expectations.

Out of Control

The illusion of control extends to relationships as well. Many self-help books offer advice on managing and influencing others, implying that you can control how people think and feel about you. While communication skills and empathy can improve relationships, you cannot control another person's feelings or actions. People are autonomous with their own thoughts, feelings, and free will. Trying to control others can lead to manipulation and disappointment.

Healthy relationships are built on mutual respect and under-standing, not control. By focusing on effective communication and empathy, you can foster stronger connections with others without attempting to dictate their behavior. Recognizing and accepting the autonomy of others can lead to more genuine and fulfilling relationships.

Health and wellness are also areas where the illusion of control is prevalent. Books promoting specific diets, exercise regimens, and lifestyle changes often promise optimal health and longevity. While taking care of your body is essential, believing that you can completely control your health ignores factors like genetics, environmental influences, and random events. Even the most health-conscious individuals can face health issues. The pressure to control every aspect of health can lead to anxiety and obsessive behaviors rather than genuine well-being.

The pursuit of health perfection can also foster a sense of inadequacy and perpetuate unrealistic beauty standards. The emphasis on achieving an ideal body shape or following a perfect diet can overshadow the importance of overall well-being and self-acceptance. It's crucial to approach health with a balanced perspective, focusing on sustainable habits and self-care rather than striving for unattainable ideals.

Regarding financial success, the self-help industry often suggests that prosperity is just a mindset away. While certain practices can improve financial situations, the idea that anyone can become wealthy through sheer willpower is misleading. Economic mobility is influenced by education, social networks, systemic inequalities, and luck. Not acknowledging these factors can lead to feelings of shame and guilt.

The financial success myth can lead individuals to believe that their financial struggles are solely due to personal failings rather than broader systemic factors. Understanding the complexities of economic mobility can help individuals adopt a more nuanced view of financial success and develop strategies that address both personal and external challenges.

Career advancement is another area where the illusion of control appears. Self-help literature often emphasizes that with the right strategies, you can achieve career success. While strategic thinking and hard work are crucial, they are not foolproof. Office politics, market conditions, and organizational culture all play significant roles. Believing you can control your career path entirely can lead to burnout and disappointment. Careers are often marked by periods of uncertainty and change. The pursuit of a perfect career path can overshadow the value of adaptability and continuous learning. Many envision career success as a linear path—one clear, upward trajectory without setbacks or deviations—but this expectation is rarely the reality. Embracing career development as an ongoing journey rather than a linear progression can lead to greater satisfaction and resilience in the face of challenges.

Mental health is another aspect where self-help literature sometimes oversimplifies. The idea that mental health issues can be overcome purely through positive thinking and self-discipline is an oversimplification. Mental health is influenced by biological, psychological, and social factors. While mindset and self-care are important, professional help and sometimes medication are necessary for many individuals. This oversimplification of mental health challenges in self-help literature can perpetuate stigma and discourage individuals from seeking appropriate care. Acknowledging the multifaceted nature of mental health can lead to a more compassionate approach and promote access to comprehensive support and treatment options.

Allure of Certainty

Why do we buy into self-help's false promises? Part of it is human nature—we crave certainty and control in an unpredictable world. Self-help books offer a comforting illusion that we can master our lives if we follow the right steps. However, this sets us up for failure by promoting unrealistic expectations.

The allure of control and mastery can be particularly strong in a world that often feels chaotic and uncertain. Self-help literature capitalizes on this desire by presenting simple solutions to complex problems. Recognizing the limitations of these promises can help individuals approach self-help with a more critical and balanced perspective.

Embracing the reality that we can't control everything means focusing on what we can—our actions, attitudes, and responses—while accepting that some things are beyond our influence. This approach can lead to healthier, more sustainable personal growth. It allows us to pursue our goals with determination and resilience, without the unrealistic expectation of total control.

Acknowledging our limitations can also foster a greater sense of humility and acceptance. It helps us navigate life with a more realistic outlook, reducing the pressure to achieve unattainable standards. This shift in perspective can lead to a more compassionate and balanced approach to personal development.

Recognizing the limits of our control can also foster compassion for ourselves and others. It helps us understand that setbacks and failures often involve factors beyond our control, reducing self-blame. It encourages mutual support in facing challenges.

Perfectibility

The self-help industry often promotes the idea of perfectibility—suggesting that perfection is within reach if we follow the right steps, adopt the correct mindset, or purchase the latest book. This illusion sets unrealistic standards, leading to disappointment and frustration. Let's examine how the pursuit of perfection, especially in love relationships, can be more harmful than helpful.

Many self-help books and experts suggest that with the right techniques, you can find your perfect partner—your "soulmate" or "Mr. Right." The idea is that if you work hard enough on yourself, you'll attract someone who meets all your criteria. But Mr. Perfect doesn't exist. What does exist is Mr. Real, and he's likely a far better match than any idealized version you have.

Fixating on perfection in a partner might lead you to dismiss potential relationships that don't meet your high standards. You may pass up opportunities to get to know Mr. Real, who might have flaws but also genuine qualities that make a relationship work. Instead of seeking someone who meets every criterion, focus on finding someone who complements your life, shares your values, and can grow with you.

When fixated on perfection, you set yourself up for failure. Every person will fall short because humans are inherently imperfect. This pursuit can result in fleeting relationships or none at all, often leaving you feeling lonely and confused. Instead, focus on finding someone who complements your life, shares your values, and meets you where you are.

In personal achievements, the illusion of perfectibility is equally damaging. Self-help literature often sets high standards for success, suggesting that you can achieve it all—career success, financial wealth, a perfect body, and a thriving social life. While aspiring to these things is admirable, the pressure to achieve perfection can be overwhelming.

Consider the idea of a "perfect" career. Self-help books often suggest that with the right strategies, you can climb to the top or start a successful business. However, careers aren't that straight forward; they are filled with ups and downs, unexpected opportunities, and setbacks. The relentless pursuit of perfection can lead to burnout and a sense of failure. Instead, focus on growth, continuous learning, and resilience. Embrace grit—keep going when it's tough, and trust that with time, the rest will fall into place.

Perfectionism

The fitness and wellness industry promotes an ideal body image that can be impossible to achieve, showcasing perfectly toned bodies and messaging that suggests following a specific regimen will help us attain the same look. This creates unrealistic expectations and can lead to unhealthy behaviors. Health and fitness should focus on feeling good and taking care of your body, rather than striving for an unattainable standard. Social media amplifies this illusion of perfectibility, presenting curated highlights instead of real struggles, which can lead to feelings of inadequacy and the pressure to portray a flawless version of oneself. It's important to recognize that behind these polished images are real people with real problems, which can help manage expectations and shift the focus back to your personal journey.

Similarly, perfectionism significantly influences how we navigate our daily lives. Self-help books often advocate for highly structured routines and productivity hacks, which can be beneficial but also create pressure to achieve a perfectly optimized life. This relentless pursuit can be exhausting. Instead, allow yourself the flexibility to embrace imperfections; doing so will foster a more carefree and satisfying perspective on life.

Perfectionism can also manifest in the quest for a "perfect" daily routine. Self-help literature often promotes rigorous schedules and productivity techniques, suggesting that adhering to these can lead to optimal efficiency and happiness. However, this approach can create undue stress and a sense of failure when life inevitably disrupts even the most well-laid plans. Embracing flexibility and allowing room for spontaneity can lead to a more balanced and fulfilling life.

Alternative to Perfectibility

Embrace imperfection and find contentment in the messiness of life. This doesn't mean settling for mediocrity but recognizing that perfection is an illusion and that striving for it can prevent you from appreciating what you have. Set realistic goals, celebrate progress, and be kind to yourself when things don't go perfectly.

In relationships, seek Mr. Real rather than Mr. Perfect. Appreciate your partner's quirks and flaws and understand that they are part of what makes them unique and lovable. Be open to growth and change together, rather than looking for an unrealistic ideal.

In your personal life, set attainable goals and acknowledge that success is not a straight path. Take care of your body because it feels good, not because of a media standard. Find balance between structure and spontaneity, and understand that life is messy and unpredictable.

Embracing imperfection allows us to experience life more fully and authentically. It encourages us to focus on meaningful experiences and personal growth. This perspective fosters resilience, creativity, and a deeper appreciation for the present moment.

The illusion of perfectibility in self-help can be enticing but also misleading. By shifting our focus from perfection to authenticity, we build a more fulfilling and balanced life. Appreciate yourself and others for who you/they are, imperfections and all. Embracing imperfection isn't about giving up on growth; it's about finding joy in the journey.

The Bhagavad Gita offers an interesting perspective on control. Krishna advises Arjuna to focus on his actions but not stress about the results. It's about doing your duty without obsessing over outcomes. This approach helps us stay grounded and less stressed about uncontrollable factors. This wisdom encourages us to act with dedication and integrity while relinquishing attachment to the results. It allows us to navigate life's challenges with composure and resilience. By focusing on our actions and intentions, we can cultivate a sense of purpose and fulfillment, regardless of external outcomes.

In essence, the pursuit of control and perfection in self-help often leads us astray. By accepting the limits of our control and the reality of imperfection, we can achieve a more fulfilling life. Recognizing and embracing our limitations fosters personal growth, resilience, and a more compassionate approach to ourselves and others.

The self-help industry's tendency to prioritize self-centered narratives often emphasizes individual perfection and achievement. While self-help can provide valuable insights for personal development, it frequently overlooks essential elements like imperfection, authenticity, and community.

PART 2.
THE SOLUTION

"The best way to find yourself is to lose yourself in the service of others."

Mahatma Gandhi

CHAPTER 8

ALTERNATIVES TO MAINSTREAM SELF-HELP

In our fast-paced digital world, it's easy to become disconnected—not just from those around us, but from our own inner selves. As we scroll through curated feeds and consume self-help literature, we may find ourselves caught in the cycle of trying to navigate life's challenges alone. While these resources can offer valuable insights, they often fall short of providing the deep support we truly need.

The alternative, however, is powerful and readily available: community and connection. Engaging with others—sharing our experiences, listening to their stories, and building relationships—can foster a sense of belonging and understanding that no book can replicate. This connection serves as a reminder that we are not alone in our struggles and triumphs.

Yet, embracing community isn't always easy. It requires vulnerability, effort, and the willingness to step outside our comfort zones. It means reaching out, attending gatherings, and being present for others, even when we're preoccupied with our own challenges. But the rewards can be profound. When we come together, we create a tapestry of support that weaves resilience into our lives. By nurturing our connections, we cultivate not only a sense of purpose but also a shared strength that empowers us to navigate life's complexities together. In a world that often feels isolating, let us remember that the most significant growth often happens within the warmth of community. When faced with a problem or a challenging life obstacle, having someone to talk to can be incredibly therapeutic. Whether it's receiving advice, a different perspective, or simply a listening ear, the act of sharing our troubles can lighten the emotional load and help us get past it. Often, a shift in perspective is all we need.

Human beings are inherently social creatures. From the earliest days of our existence, we have relied on one another for survival, comfort, and companionship. While our basic survival may no longer hinge on these connections in the modern world, our mental and emotional well-being certainly does. Consider the saying, "A problem shared is a problem halved." This timeless truth highlights the power of sharing our struggles with others, as it can significantly lighten our emotional load. When we keep our worries bottled up, they often grow disproportionately large in our minds. However, by talking to a friend, family member, or even writing it down, we can begin to view our concerns more clearly and realistically. While the problem may not disappear, it often feels more manageable once it's brought into the open. As the saying goes, "We are as sick as our secrets," reminding us that the shadows of unshared troubles can distort our mental and emotional health far more than the troubles themselves.

Strong connections also provide a vital emotional outlet

and support. In times of distress, having a proverbial shoulder to cry on can be immensely comforting. It's not just about finding solutions; sometimes, we just need to feel heard and understood. This sense of connection can diminish feelings of isolation and remind us that we are not alone in our struggles. The importance of community cannot be overstated. While relationships with individuals are crucial, being part of a larger community can provide an even deeper sense of belonging and support.

One of the criticisms of self-help is that it can focus too much on the *self*. This inward focus can lead to overthinking and increased isolation. While personal growth and self-improvement are important, they shouldn't come at the expense of our connections with others.

Engaging with a community helps shift the focus away from ourselves. When we are involved in other people's lives, our own problems can seem less overwhelming. This isn't about ignoring our issues but rather putting them into perspective. By being part of a community, we can gain insights from others' experiences and see our challenges from different angles.

Furthermore, helping others can be incredibly fulfilling and can provide a sense of purpose. Volunteering or simply being there for a friend in need can take us out of our own heads and remind us of the rewards of community. The more we engage with others, the less time we spend ruminating on our problems. This engagement can be a powerful antidote to the negative mental loops we sometimes find ourselves in.

Loneliness

Research has shown that loneliness is a significant contributor to stress and can even affect our physical health. Prolonged loneliness is associated with increased levels of the stress hormone cortisol, which can lead to a variety of health issues, including high blood pressure, weakened immune function, and increased risk of chronic diseases.

One of the most poignant examples of the impact of loneliness is the phenomenon observed in elderly couples, where one spouse often dies shortly after the other. This "widowhood effect" suggests that the surviving spouse's health deteriorates rapidly due to the profound loneliness and isolation they experience after their partner's death. Studies have found that social isolation can significantly reduce life expectancy. On the other hand, strong social connections can enhance our quality of life and increase our lifespan. Engaging with a supportive community can provide emotional support, reduce stress, and promote healthier behaviors. Simply put, being connected to others is not just a nice-to-have; it's essential for our well-being.

While self-help can offer valuable tools for personal growth, it should not be the sole focus of our efforts to improve our lives. Community and connection play an equally, if not more, important role in our well-being. Building strong relationships and being part of a supportive community can provide emotional support, a sense of belonging, and help us gain perspective on our challenges. As we navigate the complexities of modern life, it's crucial to remember that we don't have to do it alone. By fostering connections with others and actively participating in our communities, we can find the support we need to thrive. The less time we spend isolated and consumed by our thoughts, the more we can engage with the world around us and live fuller, more meaningful lives. While a self-help book might offer some general advice, turning to a support group can provide you with tailored guidance and a sense of community.

For example, joining a support group or a hobby-based community can provide an outlet for shared experiences and challenges. Whether it's a local fitness class, a writing workshop, or a meditation group, these spaces allow you to connect with others who might understand your struggles and could offer valuable insights. Engaging with a community outside of work or family can provide a fresh perspective and help you feel less isolated. Even in environments that seem competitive or individualistic, there are always people who are eager to share their stories and support one another. Finding this type of external support not only helps you tackle challenges more effectively but also promotes personal growth and emotional resilience.

Imagine someone navigating the painful journey of personal loss. While self-help resources may offer helpful coping strategies, they can never replace the security and comfort of a close friend or professional who simply sits with you, listens, and offers a supportive ear. Often, what we truly seek in these moments is to be heard and seen.

This human connection provides a level of emotional support that books and online articles simply cannot replicate. While written resources serve as appetizers, offering initial insights into healing, the true nourishment comes from sharing our experiences with another person—whether it's a professional, a trusted family member, a friend, or even someone you meet at a support group. The key is to take action and reach out, rather than keeping those troubling thoughts bottled up inside. By opening up to others, we create the opportunity to connect on a deeper level, fostering healing and understanding that can profoundly impact our journey through any challenge.

Self-help often emphasizes the idea of self-reliance and personal responsibility. While these are important qualities, they should be balanced with an understanding of our interdependence. No one can navigate life's challenges entirely on their own. Recognizing the value of community and seeking out connections can provide a more holistic approach to personal growth and well-being. The inward focus promoted by some self-help philosophies can sometimes lead to a sense of isolation. When we are constantly analyzing ourselves and our problems, it's easy to become consumed by our own thoughts. This can create a vicious cycle of overthinking and anxiety. Engaging with others helps break this cycle. By focusing on someone else's needs or simply enjoying a shared activity, we can shift our attention away from our own worries.

This shift in focus can be incredibly liberating. It allows us to see our problems in a new light and often makes them seem less daunting. Engaging with others provides a break from the mental loops that can trap us in negative thinking. It offers a reminder that there is a world outside of our own minds and that we are part of something larger.

The idea that "community is the antidote to isolation" is supported by a growing body of research. Studies have shown that people with strong social networks are generally happier and healthier than those who are isolated. They experience lower levels of stress, better mental health, and a greater sense of purpose. These benefits are not just psychological; they have tangible effects on our physical health as well.

Isolation as Illness

Research has found that social isolation can be as harmful to our health as smoking or obesity. Loneliness is linked to a higher risk of heart disease, stroke, and premature death. In contrast, strong social connections can boost our immune system, reduce inflammation, and even improve our sleep quality. These findings highlight the profound impact that our social lives have on our overall well-being.

One particularly striking example of the importance of social connections comes from studies on the elderly. It has been observed that older adults with strong social ties live longer and have better health outcomes than those who are isolated. This is particularly evident in the "Blue Zones"— regions of the world where people live significantly longer than average. Researchers have found that one of the common factors in these areas is a strong sense of community and social support. For instance, in Okinawa, Japan, elderly residents are part of tightly-knit social groups called "moais," which provide lifelong friendship and support. These social structures are believed to contribute significantly to their longevity and quality of life. The implications of these findings are clear: fostering social connections is not just beneficial but essential to our health and well-being. Yet, in our busy, modern lives, it can be easy to neglect these important relationships. We might prioritize work, personal achievements, or self-improvement activities, often at the expense of our social lives. However, the evidence suggests that making time for our relationships should be considered an integral part of our self-care routines.

Creating and maintaining a supportive community is a thoughtful process that requires intentional effort. It begins with a genuine interest in others and a commitment to investing time in nurturing relationships. Start by assessing your existing network—consider reaching out to friends you've lost touch with, connecting with colleagues in casual settings, or prioritizing quality time with trusted family members. These foundational relationships can serve as the bedrock for a more extensive social network.

To foster a sense of community, engage in activities that encourage interaction and collaboration. Join clubs, volunteer organizations, or local interest groups where you can meet new people while participating in shared passions. This not only helps expand your network but also deepens your sense of belonging.

However, it's essential to acknowledge that forming connections doesn't come easily to everyone. Factors such as social anxiety, past experiences, or discomfort in group settings can pose challenges. If you find yourself in this position, consider starting with small, manageable steps. One-on-one conversations can feel less daunting than larger gatherings, allowing for more meaningful exchanges without the pressure of a crowd.

As you gradually build confidence and trust through these intimate interactions, you can begin to explore larger social settings at your own pace. Remember, consistency is key. Regularly engaging with others, even in small ways, can lead to a more fulfilling and supportive community over time.

It's not Easy

For those who find it particularly challenging to form connections, seeking professional help can be beneficial. Therapists and counselors can provide strategies and support for overcoming social barriers and building healthy relationships. They can also help address any underlying issues that might be contributing to feelings of isolation.

In addition to the emotional and practical support that communities provide, they also offer a sense of identity and belonging. Being part of a community gives us a sense of place and purpose. It connects us to something larger than ourselves and provides a framework within which we can navigate life's challenges. This sense of belonging is fundamental to our psychological well-being.

One of the key takeaways from the discussion on community and connection is the idea that we are not meant to go through life alone. While self-help can provide valuable tools and insights for personal growth, it should be complemented with a strong support network. Engaging with others, sharing our experiences, and being part of a community can provide a level of support and perspective that we cannot achieve on our own. The inward focus promoted by many self-help philosophies can sometimes lead to a sense of isolation. When we are constantly analyzing ourselves and our problems, it's easy to become consumed by our own thoughts. This can create a vicious cycle of overthinking and anxiety. Engaging with others helps break this cycle. By focusing on someone else's needs or simply enjoying a shared activity, we can shift our attention away from our own worries, or overthinking.

Remember the tee-shirt phrase, "Don't overthink it." This shift in focus can be incredibly liberating. It allows us to see our problems in a new light and often makes them seem less daunting. Engaging with others provides a break from the mental loops that can trap us in negative thinking. It offers a reminder that there is a world outside of our own minds and that we are part of something larger.

The concept of "community and connection as an antidote" is increasingly supported by research. Studies indicate that individuals with strong social networks tend to be happier and healthier than those who are isolated. For instance, a 2018 study published in *The Journal of Happiness Studies* highlighted that the quality of social relationships is more crucial than their quantity, and meaningful connections are associated with greater life satisfaction. People with these supportive relationships experience lower stress levels, enhanced mental health, and a heightened sense of purpose. Moreover, the benefits of strong social ties extend beyond psychological well-being; they also have tangible positive effects on our physical health.

While self-help can provide valuable tools for personal growth, it is not a substitute for the support and connection that comes from being part of a community. Engaging with others, sharing our experiences, and building meaningful relationships are essential components of a fulfilling and resilient life.

As we invest in our communities and strengthen our social connections, we not only enhance our own well-being but also contribute to the well-being of those around us. In fostering a sense of community and prioritizing connection, we create a supportive network that can help us navigate life's challenges, celebrate our successes, and find meaning and purpose in our shared experiences.

In doing so, we move beyond the limitations of self-help and embrace the power of human connection, which is, ultimately, the foundation of a happy and healthy life.

CHAPTER 9
FINDING YOUR PURPOSE

An answer to the self-help dilemma might lie in shifting our focus away from ourselves and toward others. Real fulfillment perhaps begins when we shift our focus outward and is fueled by a desire to give, grow, and share—not for applause or recognition, but for the genuine, lasting impact our actions can have on others.

Service and altruism are transformative drivers of personal growth, offering benefits that ripple far beyond the immediate act. By helping others, we create meaningful change in their lives while gaining a sense of purpose and perspective ourselves. Acts of service provide a reprieve from our own worries, fostering resilience, gratitude, and a stronger connection to the world around us. And let's not underestimate the simple truth—it feels profoundly good to do good.

Performing acts of kindness trigger the release of endorphins—our brain's natural mood boosters—creating what's often called the "helper's high." This sense of euphoria and satisfaction not only feels good but also validates us on a deeper level. Altruistic behavior is also recognized and appreciated by others, which can enhance our self-esteem and sense of worth. While some may see this as selfish, it undeniably contributes to our happiness. Beyond the immediate feel-good effect, acts of service have a tangible impact on society. Communities thrive when people actively support one another, creating a wave that inspires others to do the same. These collective efforts strengthen societal bonds and foster a culture of mutual care. Knowing that our actions contribute to the greater good provides a sense of purpose and belonging, reinforcing our commitment to compassion and service.

To truly escape excessive self-focus and experience the real rewards of serving others, you need to measure the inconvenience it causes you. Genuine service often involves stepping beyond minor gestures, like holding a door open—which, while kind, is rarely transformative. The real test of service is when it genuinely inconveniences you. Cleaning up someone's poop or puke, for example, is uncomfortable and unpleasant, but it's in these moments of true inconvenience that the act becomes meaningful. If your service doesn't disrupt your comfort or routine, it's likely benefiting you more than the other person. True service demands effort, sacrifice, and a willingness to put others' needs ahead of your own. And that's not easy.

Engaging in acts of service has a remarkable way of shifting our focus. When we do something for someone else, our own worries often fade, providing a much-needed mental break. Service also broadens our perspective, reminding us of the blessings we might otherwise take for granted. Witnessing the challenges others face and offering support can inspire gratitude and contentment, grounding us in a sense of appreciation for what we have.

Service isn't just a tool for personal growth; it can also be transformative in resolving conflicts. Our instinct during arguments is often to react with anger or defensiveness, but adopting a service-oriented mindset can completely change the dynamic. Instead of responding with hostility, ask yourself how you can be of service in the situation. This shift in perspective helps depersonalize the conflict, allowing you to approach it with empathy and a focus on solutions rather than blame. By prioritizing understanding over winning, you're more likely to diffuse tension and reach a resolution that respects both sides. Serving the situation rather than dominating it turns the focus from conflict to collaboration, opening the door to a more positive outcome for everyone involved.

Service is a powerful tool for both personal and professional growth. Mentoring colleagues, sharing expertise, or offering support during challenging projects not only strengthens workplace relationships but also enhances leadership skills. By investing in the growth and success of others, we foster a positive work environment that benefits everyone involved. The impact of such contributions can be deeply fulfilling, often leading to career advancement and a stronger sense of purpose.

Often in the workplace, it's not just the quality of your work that gets noticed, but how you collaborate, support, and help others. These actions tend to leave a lasting impression on colleagues and leadership alike. Remember, people buy into people—they respond to kindness, teamwork, and genuine efforts to uplift those around them. Career advancement is often driven more by how you interact with and support others than by staying late to finish a report or making a solo contribution to a project. Keep in mind: the way you show up for your team can matter more than the specific task you complete.

Incorporating service into daily life doesn't require grand gestures or significant time commitments. Small, consistent acts of kindness—such as sending an encouraging message to a friend or offering assistance to a colleague—can have a profound effect. These simple actions set a positive tone for the day and inspire others to do the same, creating a chain of goodwill and connection.

Service plays a critical role in building resilience too. Life's challenges are inevitable, but focusing on the needs of others provides stability and a renewed sense of purpose during tough times. When we help others, our own struggles often feel more manageable. Acts of service shift our perspective, enabling us to navigate adversity with greater strength and clarity. Moreover, through helping, we form connections that offer support, encouragement, and practical assistance—essential tools for overcoming our own obstacles.

Helping others deepens this sense of connection by fostering a profound awareness of our interconnectedness. When we recognize the ripple effect of our actions, we are reminded that we are part of a larger community. This understanding enhances our sense of belonging and diminishes feelings of isolation. It reinforces the comforting truth that we are never truly alone in our struggles and underscores our power to create meaningful change in the lives of others. In giving, we not only uplift those around us but also find resilience and purpose within ourselves.

Acts of service can be transformative, pushing us out of our comfort zones and into engagement with diverse communities.

These experiences challenge our assumptions, broaden our perspectives, and spark personal growth. They can also inspire new passions and interests, enriching our lives in unexpected ways. Even small acts of kindness contribute to a culture of empathy and support, strengthening the bonds within our communities and fostering a more compassionate, connected world.

Service as the Solution

The way we treat others also reflects how we treat ourselves. Incorporating service into your life can be a transformative antidote to feelings of inadequacy or low self-esteem. When you focus on helping others, you naturally shift from self-doubt to a sense of accomplishment and worth. This shift can be deeply empowering, as seeing the tangible results of your efforts and receiving appreciation from those you help reinforces your sense of purpose and builds confidence. If you struggle with low self-esteem, start by engaging in esteemable acts—small, meaningful gestures of kindness and support. These actions not only uplift others but also serve as a powerful reminder of your own value.

Service is a critical component of building and sustaining relationships, as acts of service create opportunities for meaningful interactions and strengthen bonds with others. Whether through shared work, community projects, or simply being there for a friend in need, these experiences foster trust and mutual respect. Over time, such connections become a vital support network, providing comfort and assistance during difficult times.

Moreover, the principle that "you get back what you give"

highlights the cyclical nature of service. Acts of kindness set a precedent for others to follow, cultivating a culture of compassion and support. When people witness acts of service, they are often inspired to contribute in their own way. This cycle fosters a more cooperative community, where individuals look out for one another and work together toward common goals.

By integrating service into our lives, we not only enhance our personal relationships but also contribute to the well-being of the broader community. This approach leads to a more interconnected and supportive society, benefiting all its members.

Engaging in acts of kindness and support can be therapeutic, helping to alleviate feelings of grief, loss, or trauma. When we help others, we often find a sense of purpose and meaning that can be deeply healing. It allows us to transform our pain into positive action, creating a legacy of resilience and strength.

It's also a pathway to gratitude. When we help others, especially those less fortunate, we become more aware of our own privilege and resources. This awareness can cultivate a deep sense of gratitude and contentment. It shifts our focus from what we lack to what we have, fostering a more positive and appreciative outlook on life. Engaging in service activities can also broaden our perspective. It encourages us to consider the wider impact of our actions and to strive for outcomes that benefit the greater good.

So, when you're feeling stuck or overwhelmed, remember that one of the best ways out of your over thinking might just be through helping someone else. Service and altruism aren't just about being kind; they're powerful, almost selfish tools for enhancing our own well-being while simultaneously creating a better world. By putting our energy into supporting others, we often find that we're lifting ourselves up in the process.

The Pursuit of Better

In a world where self-improvement has become an industry unto itself, promising to unlock our full potential, it's easy to get caught up in the relentless pursuit of a "better" version of ourselves.

However, there are healthier alternatives to this constant quest for self-betterment—alternatives that emphasize being present and embracing who we are at this moment. Contemplation and acceptance are two powerful ideas that can serve as healthier alternatives to the often excessive self-improvement encouraged by self-help culture. Together, they provide a balanced approach: contemplation helps us understand ourselves and our actions with clarity, while acceptance allows us to see and embrace the world as it is, rather than as we wish it to be.

When practiced together, contemplation and acceptance create a powerful synergy. Contemplation encourages us to look inward and understand our role in shaping our lives, while acceptance teaches us to find peace with the things we cannot control. This dual approach nurtures both self-awareness and resilience, leading to a healthier, more balanced way of engaging with ourselves and the world.

These practices remind us that growth doesn't come from constant self-criticism or the endless pursuit of improvement but from a grounded, compassionate understanding of ourselves and an open-hearted embrace of reality.

Developing the Right Attitude

Mindfulness, at its core, is the practice of being present in the moment. It involves paying attention to our thoughts, feelings, and surroundings without judgment. This practice aims to declutter the mind rather than fill it, fostering clarity and focus. The term "mindfulness" is often misunderstood; it's not about having a "mind full" of thoughts but about achieving a state of "mindful" awareness. This distinction highlights that mindfulness is about emptying the mind of unnecessary clutter to fully engage with the present. In our efforts to become more mindful, we often find ourselves adding more activities to our already busy lives and minds: mindfulness apps, self-improvement online courses, self-help books, and more. But true mindfulness is about simplifying and focusing on the present rather than complicating our routines—it's actually about being "mindful-less."

Meditation is a common mindfulness practice, often depicted as sitting on a cushion, breathing deeply, and trying to clear the mind of thoughts. While this is a popular approach, it is by no means the only way to meditate. In fact, meditation can be integrated into nearly any activity. Walking meditations, for instance, involve paying attention to the sensations of each step, the feel of the ground underfoot, and the rhythm of your breathing as you move. Listening to music can also be a form of meditation when we fully immerse ourselves in the sounds, allowing the music to wash over us and freeing our minds from the "bad weather" of distracting thoughts.

Physical activities like working out, running, or cycling can also serve as meditative practice. In those moments when we are deeply engaged in our movements—lost in the rhythm and magic of the activity—we experience a powerful form of meditation. This focus on the act itself shifts our attention away from the "self," helping us escape the turbulence and chatter of our everyday minds. When we jog and concentrate on our breath, the rhythm of our feet hitting the pavement, and the scenery around us, we are actively practicing mindfulness. Likewise, a long bike ride or a hike in nature can become a meditative experience when we are fully present and attuned to our surroundings and nature.

For beginners, active forms of meditation can be particularly accessible and attractive. These practices do not require the ability to sit still for long periods or to try and clear the mind of all thoughts, involve no ceremony or judgment by seasoned meditators, and cost nothing. By recognizing these moments as meditation, we can integrate mindfulness into our daily lives without feeling the need to set aside specific times for traditional practice.

One often overlooked yet powerful form of active meditation is listening. When we truly listen, we step out of our own minds and shift the focus to someone else. This simple act can help us think less about ourselves, breaking the cycle of self-centered thoughts and creating space for genuine presence.

How Listening is a Mindfulness Practice

As you focus entirely on the words, tone, and body language of the person speaking, you naturally quiet your own inner dialogue. By letting go of the urge to judge, interrupt, or form a response, you immerse yourself in the present moment, cultivating a state of mindfulness.

Be Present: Treat listening as an act of service. Shift your attention fully to the speaker, setting aside distractions and your own thoughts.

Practice Openness: Suspend judgment and resist the urge to problem-solve or offer advice. Instead, aim to understand.

Reflect Back: Show you're engaged by summarizing or reflecting what you've heard. For example, "It sounds like you're feeling overwhelmed because of..."

Embrace Silence: Allow pauses in the conversation. Silence creates space for the speaker to process and share more deeply.

For the listener, this practice fosters a sense of connection, reduces self-focused worry, and cultivates empathy. It's a moment to step outside of yourself and experience the world through someone else's perspective. For the person being listened to, the benefits are profound—they feel seen, valued, and understood. Listening deeply to others strengthens relationships and contributes to a sense of mutual presence and trust.

Mindfulness practices are more accessible than ever, offering a range of approaches to suit different needs and lifestyles. Apps like Calm provide guided meditations for stress relief, improved focus, and better sleep, making mindfulness approachable for beginners and seasoned practitioners alike. For those seeking free resources, YouTube offers a wealth of options. Creators like Tara Brach share meditations centered on compassion and presence, while Michael Sealey focuses on relaxation techniques designed to ease stress and promote restful sleep. The beauty of meditation is that it's accessible to everyone, and there are plenty of free resources to help you get started. The key is to take that first step and remember why it's called a "practice"—because it's an ongoing journey of learning and refinement. Be patient with yourself as you embrace it.

While self-help gurus often overcomplicate meditation, making it seem like a skill requiring expensive training or retreats, it doesn't have to be that way. Meditation can be as simple as focusing on your breath or, just as effectively, listening deeply to others. These straightforward practices can be just as impactful as more elaborate methods.

It's also important to understand that the purpose of meditation or active listening isn't necessarily to feel good. It's not about chasing moments of bliss or calm but about cultivating a state of presence. These practices prepare us to show up in the world more attuned, grounded, and ready to engage with others meaningfully. They are not simply self-serving—they enable us to connect with and contribute positively to the world around us. Listening and meditation, in their purest forms, are among the simplest yet most profound ways to do just that.

CHAPTER 10
SELF-ACCEPTANCE IS THE ANSWER

The idea of acceptance is about embracing reality as it is, without resistance or judgment. It's about recognizing that while we may not have control over everything that happens to us, we do have control over how we respond or react. So acceptance could perhaps be one answer to handling many of our problems.

Acceptance doesn't mean resignation or giving up. Instead, it involves acknowledging our circumstances and finding peace with them, whatever they may be and however painful they are. When we accept our current situation, we stop fighting against it and allow ourselves to move forward with greater clarity and calm. Acceptance can be applied to various aspects of our lives, from our emotions and thoughts to our relationships and major life events.

For instance, if we are experiencing sadness or frustration, acceptance involves acknowledging these emotions without trying to suppress or change them. By allowing ourselves to fully experience our emotions, we can move through them more effectively. Perhaps we can even view them as energy—transient forces that flow through us, guiding our experiences rather than defining them. This process can be incredibly liberating, as it removes the additional burden of resisting our natural responses.

In relationships, acceptance can play a crucial role in reducing conflict and fostering harmony. Instead of trying to change our partners or friends, we can accept them as they are, with all their imperfections and quirks. This doesn't mean we tolerate harmful behavior, but it does mean we approach our relationships with empathy and understanding. By accepting others, we create a space for genuine connection and mutual respect. The concept of acceptance also applies to other life circumstances. There will always be situations beyond our control—loss, illness, disappointment, and uncertainty. Acceptance allows us to face these challenges with grace and resilience. It involves letting go of the need for things to be different and finding peace in the present moment. One of the most profound aspects of acceptance is its ability to bring us peace.

When we stop resisting reality, we release a significant amount of mental and emotional tension. This shift in perspective can be transformative. Instead of being caught up in what should or shouldn't be, we can focus on what is and how we can navigate it. Acceptance doesn't eliminate challenges, but it changes how we experience them.

Building on our exploration of mindfulness and acceptance in the last chapter, it's important to recognize that they both go hand in hand. Mindfulness teaches us to be present, while acceptance encourages us to embrace that present moment, regardless of what it may bring. Together, they provide a powerful antidote to the constant striving and self-criticism that often accompany self-improvement efforts. Instead of relentlessly seeking to be better, mindfulness and acceptance invite us to be fully ourselves, right here and now. Self-acceptance becomes the foundation of a peaceful and fulfilling life. These practices remind us that we are enough as we are and that true growth comes from within.

Rather than getting caught up in the never-ending pursuit of self-improvement, let's focus on being present and accepting ourselves. This simple shift can lead to profound personal growth and a deeper sense of contentment.

Just Let Go

Expanding on the concept of acceptance, we should consider incorporating spirituality and, importantly, examining how it differs from religion. Spiritual practice is not confined to a specific set of beliefs or rituals; it transcends religious boundaries, tapping into a deeper sense of seeking, trusting, and letting go. People on a spiritual path often arrive at a state of awareness through personal struggles—whether it's a breakdown or significant life challenges—that compel them to reflect deeply and cultivate gratitude. Unlike those who fear damnation in religious contexts, these individuals have faced their own versions of hell and emerged with a renewed perspective on life. Religious people don't want to go to hell. Spiritual people have already been there.

The spiritual journey involves looking inward to connect with something greater than ourselves. It requires letting go of our ego and the desire to control everything, surrendering instead to a higher power or the natural flow of the universe. This journey fosters a sense of peace and acceptance, guiding us toward a more fulfilling existence.

The act of letting go is inherently spiritual. It involves releasing our grip on the need to control outcomes and trusting that things will unfold as they should. This surrender is not about giving up but about finding peace in the uncertainty and trusting a process greater than ourselves. Whether it's letting go of a relationship, a job, or a long-held belief, this act opens us up to new possibilities and a deeper sense of mental freedom.

Any act of selflessness can be seen as spiritual. When we help others without expecting anything in return, we connect with the essence of what it means to be human. These moments of connection transcend the ego, tapping into a profound sense of universal compassion and love. Volunteering, offering support to a friend in need, or engaging in simple acts of kindness are tangible ways to bring spirituality into our everyday lives.

In this context, seeking and trusting in spirit reflects our innate desire for connection, meaning, and understanding beyond the material world. It invites us to trust the unfolding of life and recognize the presence of a greater power—whether that power is God, the universe, or the collective energy of all beings. Spirituality encourages us to surrender the illusion of control and embrace this deeper, interconnected flow of existence. Perhaps, to accept everything as it is, recognizing that it is likely how it should be.

Astrology, too, can be considered a spiritual practice. By looking to the stars and planets for guidance and understanding, we acknowledge forces at work beyond our control. Astrology encourages us to accept our place in the universe and trust in its influence over our lives. It's about seeking wisdom and trusting that the cosmos has a plan, even if we don't fully understand it.

At its core, spirituality is less about the self and more about our connection to something greater. When we shift our focus from self-centered pursuits to a broader perspective, we align more deeply with spiritual principles. This shift can lead to a more fulfilling and peaceful life as we learn to navigate our existence with trust and humility.

A spiritual solution is both profound and accessible. It's not about adhering to strict religious doctrines but rather about seeking, trusting, and letting go. Spirituality offers a clear pathway to inner peace and personal growth. The less we focus on ourselves and the more we open up to the world around us, the more spiritual our lives become. That journey involves embracing the unknown, finding strength in vulnerability, and recognizing our part in something much larger than ourselves. The key is to tap into that connection and trust the process.

CHAPTER 11

THE SECRETS OF SELF CONTROL

Self-control is one of those terms we often hear but rarely stop to define. At its core, self-control is the ability to regulate one's emotions, thoughts, and behavior in the face of temptations and impulses. It is the foundation of personal growth and success. Think about it, achieving long-term goals, maintaining healthy relationships, a successful career, and leading a balanced life all hinge on our ability to control our impulses and make thoughtful decisions.

When discussing self-control, it's essential to first examine the "self"—who or what it truly is. When posed with the question, "Who am I?" Michael Singer would answer, "You are the awareness," or "the one that sees." In the context of self-control, I interpret this as being conscious of my actions, thoughts, and reactions without being dominated by them. True self-control arises from this heightened awareness—when I am fully present and awake to what unfolds within and around me.

A common misconception about self-control is that it's solely about willpower or abstinence; we often think it's simply about not doing something or avoiding it altogether. We've all heard the phrase "just have more willpower," as if it's a muscle we can flex at will. However, research suggests that self-control is much more nuanced than that. Willpower is just one part of the equation, and relying on it alone can often lead to massive frustration and failure.

The key lies in learning to delay—or at least recognize—that you are wanting or desiring something. Awareness should always be the first step. By pausing to observe the craving or impulse, we create space to make a more thoughtful choice instead of reacting automatically. This shift in approach transforms self-control from a battle of sheer willpower into a skill of mindful response.

Self-control involves a combination of strategies and practices that help us manage our behavior and emotions effectively.

The Science

To understand self-control, it's helpful to look at the science behind it. The prefrontal cortex, a part of the brain located just behind the forehead, plays a crucial role. This area, specifically the ventromedial prefrontal cortex, is responsible for higher-order functions such as decision-making, problem-solving, and impulse control. When we exercise self-control, the prefrontal cortex is actively working to override our immediate desires and focus on long-term goals. Neuroplasticity, the brain's ability to reorganize itself by forming new neural connections, also plays a role. This means that with practice, we can strengthen our self-control abilities.

One of the most famous studies on self-control is the Marshmallow Test, conducted by psychologist Walter Mischel in the 1960s. In this experiment, children were given a choice: they could eat one marshmallow immediately or wait 15 minutes and receive two marshmallows. The researchers found that children who were able to wait tended to have better life outcomes, including higher academic achievement and better health. This study highlighted the importance of delayed gratification, a key component of self-control. Delayed gratification is crucial because it helps us prioritize long-term benefits over immediate pleasure, leading to more sustainable success and well-being.

Just like learning a new skill, developing self-control requires consistent effort and practice. Like going to the gym, it takes time to build muscle. Psychologist Kelly McGonigal emphasizes the importance of building self control through small, manageable steps. In her book *The Willpower Instinct*, she introduces the "pause and plan" technique: when faced with temptation, take a moment to pause, consider the long-term benefits of resisting, and plan your response. This approach helps rewire your brain to make more thoughtful choices over time, making her book a great resource for understanding how to train and improve self-control.

Make It Happen

Self-control isn't just a concept; it's a practical skill we draw upon every day. Whether it's maintaining a healthy diet, limiting social media use, sticking to an exercise routine, or staying productive at work, self-control plays a critical role. Yet, it's often easier said than done. Cravings for unhealthy foods, the lure of Instagram validation, or the temptation to skip workouts when tired all test our resolve, especially when we expect immediate results.

Willpower alone is fragile and inconsistent, particularly when faced with repeated temptations. A more effective approach is to design environments that support our goals. For example, preparing healthy meals in advance reduces the likelihood of reaching for junk food when hunger strikes. Similarly, keeping distractions out of your workspace or using apps to limit social media can make staying on track easier. By proactively shaping our surroundings, we ease the burden on willpower and create a foundation for consistent, sustainable progress.

Intentional awareness is another powerful tool for enhancing self-control. Focusing on small, achievable wins instead of drastic changes can build momentum and reinforce self-discipline. Celebrating each positive choice, no matter how minor, strengthens the habit of making thoughtful decisions. Over time, true transformation emerges not just from exerting self-control but from combining supportive environments with conscious, deliberate actions.

In professional settings, self-control is key to maintaining focus and achieving long-term goals. Procrastination, a common challenge, can often be addressed through simple strategies like the Pomodoro Technique, developed by Francesco Cirillo in the late 1980s. Named after the tomato-shaped kitchen timer Cirillo used as a university student, the method involves working in focused 25-minute intervals (Pomodoros), followed by 5-minute breaks. After completing four Pomodoros, a longer break of 15–30 minutes is taken. This approach helps sustain concentration, prevent long term burnout, and improve productivity by breaking tasks into manageable chunks, reducing reliance on sheer willpower.

In relationships—whether professional or personal—self-control plays a pivotal role in managing emotions and fostering effective communication. While anger and frustration are natural, acting impulsively can escalate conflicts and damage trust. A disagreement can spiral if both parties respond with anger—fueling a cycle of negativity. Instead, creating a pause between the impulse and the reaction, such as deep breathing or a brief moment of reflection, allows for calmer, more thoughtful responses. This space not only de-escalates tension but also nurtures healthier, more supportive connections.

Practicing delayed gratification is another form of self-control that strengthens our ability to resist temptations. It involves consciously waiting for a more meaningful reward rather than opting for immediate pleasure—saving for a larger purchase instead of impulsive spending or postponing a treat to savor it later. Interestingly, anticipation can sometimes be as satisfying as the reward itself. For example, vividly imagining the perfect donut—its enticing aroma, the mix of soft and crunchy textures, and the sweet taste combined with a hint of saltiness—can elicit a sense of satisfaction that may even surpass the actual act of eating it.

Ultimately, self-control is not about constant restraint but about creating conditions that make it easier to choose wisely. By designing environments that align with our goals, cultivating intentional awareness, and practicing delayed gratification, we can navigate life's challenges with greater ease and achieve lasting growth.

Triggers

Everyone faces challenges with self-control, and the key to over-coming these obstacles is recognizing them, which takes time and practice. Noticing triggers and identifying the situations and emotions that challenge our self-control is the first step in managing them.

By identifying these triggers, we can develop strategies to address them before they lead to impulsive actions. For instance, during conflicts, recognizing that factors like tiredness, hunger, anger, or loneliness might be influencing our reactions allows us to pause, take a deep breath, and approach the situation more thoughtfully. The key is to avoid believing every thought that arises and to resist the urge to react impulsively.

To manage stress and resist temptation effectively, it's important to cultivate coping strategies. These might include practices such as deep breathing, meditation, taking a walk, journaling, or talking to someone you trust. Having a well-rounded "toolbox" of techniques empowers us to navigate challenging situations with greater clarity and resilience. Sharing your thoughts with a trusted friend, therapist, or family member can also provide relief and valuable perspective, helping you process emotions and avoid rash reactions. Similarly, journaling can serve as a constructive outlet for self-reflection and emotional release. By regularly incorporating these strategies into your routine, you can better handle difficulties and maintain emotional balance.

Self-control is like a muscle that strengthens with consistent practice. By regularly exercising self-discipline and learning from setbacks, we build the capacity to manage impulses over time. Crucially, it's important to approach slip-ups with self-compassion rather than criticism. When we give in to an impulse—such as eating half the cake instead of just a slice—

acknowledging the behavior is the crucial first step toward making a change. Instead of berating ourselves, we can reflect on what happened, identify triggers, and plan more effective strategies for the future.

Balancing self-control with self-compassion is essential for long-term success. Mistakes are inevitable—whether it's missing a workout, losing our temper, or making a choice we regret. What truly matters is how we respond. Seeing setbacks as opportunities for growth, rather than reasons for self-criticism, enables us to reset and progress with greater clarity. One slip-up doesn't define us; each day offers a fresh opportunity to get back on track and continue strengthening our resilience.

Lead the Way

Mahatma Gandhi's unwavering commitment to nonviolence and self-discipline in the face of adversity exemplifies the profound influence of self-control when paired with a clear moral vision. His ability to adhere to the principles of Satyagraha—truth and nonviolence—even under immense pressure and personal sacrifice, was not merely about restraint but a deeply intentional alignment of his actions with his values. Gandhi's self-control allowed him to channel frustration and pain into constructive, peaceful resistance, uniting millions and driving transformative societal change. It was his discipline, combined with an unshakable belief in the power of nonviolence, that enabled him to lead a movement capable of dismantling colonial rule and inspiring global movements for justice.

In stark contrast, figures like Vladimir Putin appear to operate from a place of unresolved inner conflict, shaped by personal frustrations, childhood trauma, and fear. Such emotional undercurrents can manifest in destructive choices that prioritize domination over collaboration and fear over understanding. This contrast underscores the idea that self-control without self-awareness—or worse, when driven by unacknowledged inner turmoil—can lead to harm. Unlike Gandhi, whose self-discipline served a higher purpose of unity and progress, actions rooted in unresolved anger or fear often perpetuate cycles of destruction, highlighting the critical importance of understanding oneself and the impact of one's choices on others.

Michael Phelps' journey to becoming the most decorated Olympian of all time is indeed a testament to extraordinary self-control, but his success extends beyond discipline and grit—it's a story of resilience, adaptability, and mental fortitude. His rigorous training regimen, which involved waking before dawn, swimming up to five miles daily, and adhering to a strict diet and recovery routine, showcases the discipline required for such achievements. However, Phelps' success was not just physical; it was deeply rooted in his ability to manage the mental and emotional challenges that came with high-stakes competition.

To handle anxiety and pressure, Phelps incorporated visualization, controlled breathing exercises, and positive self-talk into his preparation. These techniques not only helped him stay present and focused but also allowed him to visualize success in vivid detail, which became a cornerstone of his performance strategy. Establishing pre-race routines and setting incremental goals provided him with structure and confidence, while the guidance of his long-time coach, Bob Bowman, ensured he stayed on track.

This demonstrates that while self-control and grit are vital, true greatness often involves addressing the whole. Phelps' story is not just about discipline but about the exchange of physical preparation, mental resilience, emotional awareness, and the support of a trusted team, all of which contributed to his unprecedented achievements.

Self-control doesn't have to be a solitary effort; in fact, community and support systems are invaluable in fostering it. A strong support network provides not only encouragement but also accountability, helping us remain aligned with our goals even when challenges arise. These connections cultivate a sense of shared responsibility, where others can offer motivation, guidance, and perspective when our resolve falters. An accountability partner can step in during moments of doubt, reigniting our commitment and reinforcing our dedication to self-discipline and growth. With the right support, self-control transforms from an isolated struggle into a collaborative and empowering journey toward success.

#Havoc

In today's digital age, self-control is more challenging than ever. The constant availability of information and entertainment can be overwhelming, making it difficult to focus and know when to stop scrolling. Managing distractions in our digital world is crucial. Social media, email, the news cycle, and other digital platforms are designed to capture our attention and keep us engaged. They want us to be hooked; they want our attention as that is where they make their money. Recognizing these distractions and setting boundaries is essential.

Strategies for managing screen time and staying focused include setting specific times for checking emails and social media, using apps that limit screen time, or deleting social apps when not using them and reloading when you want to view. That process alone will stop you from constantly wanting to scroll.

The impact of social media on self-control is profound. The constant barrage of notifications and the pressure to remain connected can undermine focus and productivity, making it challenging to prioritize other tasks. To maintain self-control, it's essential to set clear boundaries around social media usage. Tools like Freedom or StayFocusd can help by blocking access to distracting websites, allowing you to stay on track. Recognizing the issue is the first step, but taking deliberate action is what ultimately makes the difference.

By implementing strategies to limit distractions, you can regain control and create space for more meaningful activities.

Personal Growth

Ultimately, self-control is about personal growth and self-improvement. By continuously seeking to improve our self-control, we can achieve our long-term goals and lead more fulfilling lives because we are less stuck in the short term of quick fixes or instant gratification.

By understanding the science behind self-control, recognizing its importance in everyday life, and practicing techniques to enhance it, we can improve our ability to make thoughtful decisions. Balancing self-control with self-compassion, seeking support from our communities, and managing modern distractions can help us navigate the challenges of today's world. This is not just about willpower; it's about developing strategies and practices that help us manage our behavior and emotions effectively.

The journey to mastering self-control is ongoing, but by incorporating these strategies into our daily lives, we can develop greater resilience, take things less personally, and be able to move on and through life with greater ease.

CHAPTER 12

EMBRACING OUR IMPERFECTIONS

In a world that often glorifies perfection, embracing our imperfections can seem like a radical act.

Yet, it is within our imperfections that we find authenticity, growth, and true happiness. In sharing our whole selves—warts and all—we give people something real to connect with, and they genuinely want to connect with the real us. The beauty of imperfection, the pitfalls of perfectionism, and healthier approaches to traditional goal-setting are crucial elements to explore.

Perfection is an illusion. The idea that we can achieve flawlessness in any aspect of our lives is not only unrealistic but also detrimental to our well-being. Yet, we are sold the idea that life is a problem to be solved and self-help is a solution. Embracing imperfection means accepting ourselves and others as we are, with all our flaws and shortcomings. It is about recognizing that our imperfections make us unique and contribute to our growth and resilience.

In the tech world, phrases like "fail faster" or "break things and move on" have become mantras, popularized by leaders like Mark Zuckerberg. While you may not be a fan of Zuck, his perspective carries weight: progress—whether in life or work—requires a willingness to take risks, experiment, and embrace innovation. Staying open to new possibilities and learning from failure are essential components of growth and adaptability. Steve Jobs, known for his relentless pursuit of innovation, embraced imperfection and saw failure as an essential part of the creative process. Jobs once said, "The people who are crazy enough to think they can change the world are the ones who do." His willingness to take risks and learn from mistakes led to groundbreaking innovations that have transformed the tech industry.

Marianne Williamson, in her book *A Return to Love*, beautifully encapsulates the essence of embracing imperfection: "We are not perfect, but we are whole. When we accept our imperfections, we become more authentic, more real." This authenticity fosters deeper connections with others and enables us to build meaningful relationships. By accepting our flaws, we grant ourselves permission to be human, allowing for personal growth and learning from our experiences.

Perfectionism is often portrayed as a virtue, a driving force behind success and achievement. However, this is an outdated view. The relentless pursuit of perfection can have severe consequences on our mental and emotional health. It burns us out and leaves us never feeling happy or satisfied, as we remain in a world of always having to do better. Perfectionism can lead to chronic stress, anxiety, and a constant feeling of inadequacy and failure.

In her book *The Gifts of Imperfection*, Brené Brown examines the dangers of perfectionism, revealing that it is not about striving for excellence but rather about seeking approval and acceptance. She describes perfectionism as "a self-destructive and addictive belief system that fuels this primary thought: If I look perfect and do everything perfectly, I can avoid or minimize the painful feelings of shame, judgment, and blame." Brown's insights highlight how the pursuit of perfection can hinder our well-being and authentic connections with others.

Unrealistic Expectations

Perfectionism can hinder personal growth and happiness by creating unrealistic expectations and setting us up for disappointment. It can prevent us from taking risks and trying new things for fear of failure. In the long run, perfectionism stifles creativity and innovation, as we become more focused on avoiding mistakes than on exploring new possibilities.

While it is important to have clear objectives, focusing solely on the end result can be overwhelming and discouraging. Instead, shift your focus to the process and the steps you need to take to reach your goal. Remember the "One Day at a Time" mantra. Celebrate small victories along the way and acknowledge your efforts and progress. Failure is an inevitable part of the journey toward growth and improvement. Rather than viewing failure as a reflection of your worth, see it as an opportunity to learn and grow. Review what went wrong, make necessary adjustments, and move forward with greater wisdom and resilience.

Instead of striving for perfection, we should aim for progress and growth. Setting realistic and achievable goals allows us to celebrate our accomplishments and learn from our mistakes. One effective way to set goals is by using the SMART framework—Specific, Measurable, Achievable, Relevant, and Time-bound—which was first introduced by George T. Doran in 1981. Instead of setting a vague goal like "get in shape", a SMART goal would be "exercise for 30 minutes three times a week for the next three months". This approach provides clarity, structure, and motivation, making it easier to track progress and stay committed.

Be kind to yourself throughout this journey. Recognize that everyone makes mistakes and experiences setbacks. Treat yourself with the same compassion and understanding that you would offer to a friend. Self-compassion helps build resilience and encourages a positive mindset. Take it easy; easy does it. This mentality will subconsciously encourage you to keep going even when the going gets tough.

Imperfection Vs Perfection

Many authors and researchers have delved into the concept of imperfection and the pitfalls of perfectionism, offering valuable insights on embracing our flaws and fostering a healthier approach to personal growth. Dr. Kristin Neff, a pioneer in self-compassion research, underscores the significance of being kind to ourselves. In her book *Self-Compassion: The Proven Power of Being Kind to Yourself*, Neff explains that self-compassion involves treating ourselves with the same care and understanding we would extend to a friend. She writes, "When we give ourselves compassion, we are opening our hearts in a way that can transform our lives."

Elizabeth Gilbert, in her book *Big Magic: Creative Living Beyond Fear*, explores how embracing imperfection can enhance creativity. She encourages us to pursue our passions without succumbing to the fear of failure or the need for perfection. Gilbert asserts, "Perfectionism stops people from completing their work, yes—but even worse, it often stops people from beginning their work."Ultimately, she emphasizes that the most crucial step is simply starting.

Dr. Carol Dweck, a psychologist renowned for her research on mindset, examines the distinction between a fixed mindset and a growth mindset in her book *Mindset: The New Psychology of Success*. Dweck explains that individuals with a growth mindset perceive challenges and failures as opportunities for growth and learning, whereas those with a fixed mindset see them as threats to their intelligence or abilities. By embracing a growth mindset, we can appreciate our imperfections and recognize them as a natural part of the learning process.

Authenticity, rather than perfectionism, may be a better goal to strive for. When we embrace our true selves, including our flaws and imperfections, we become more relatable and genuine. Authenticity fosters deeper connections with others and creates an environment where we can thrive because we reveal something about ourselves that others can connect to.

In *A Return to Love*, Marianne Williamson addresses the power of authenticity, stating, "Our deepest fear is not that we are inadequate. Our deepest fear is that we are powerful beyond measure." By embracing our imperfections, we liberate ourselves from the constraints of perfectionism, allowing our true selves to shine.

Media mogul and philanthropist, Oprah Winfrey, has been open about her struggles and imperfections throughout her career. Her authenticity and vulnerabilities have endeared her though to millions of viewers and created a powerful connection with her audience. Winfrey's story demonstrates the strength and influence that come from embracing one's true self. She often speaks about her difficult childhood and personal challenges, showing that it is possible to overcome adversity and succeed without being perfect.

One of the main reasons we strive for perfection is the fear of judgment from others. We worry that our flaws will be exposed and that we will be seen as inadequate. Overcoming this fear requires a change in perspective. Instead of viewing imperfections as weaknesses, reframe them as opportunities for growth and connection. Allow yourself to be vulnerable and open with others. Share your struggles and imperfections, and invite others to do the same. Vulnerability builds trust and connection, and it allows us to experience the full range of human emotions.

Work on accepting yourself as you are, flaws and all. This means letting go of the need for external validation and finding contentment within yourself. Self-acceptance is a powerful antidote to the fear of judgment and a key component of embracing imperfection.

Compassion and Awareness

Compassion and empathy are essential in embracing imperfection, both in ourselves and others. When we extend compassion, we foster an environment where flaws are not only accepted but celebrated as part of the human experience. Practicing self-compassion means treating ourselves with kindness and understanding, acknowledging our imperfections without judgment, and cultivating a supportive inner dialogue. This self-acceptance lays the foundation for personal growth and resilience.

Similarly, empathy allows us to connect more deeply with others by recognizing that everyone faces struggles and imperfection. This understanding fosters greater compassion and reduces judgment, creating a culture of acceptance and mutual support. Together, compassion and empathy enable us to embrace imperfection, transforming it into a source of connection and strength.

Awareness is also a powerful tool for embracing imperfection. Being aware means being present in the moment and accepting our experiences without judgment. Practicing awareness, or mindfulness can help us become more conscious of our thoughts and emotions, allowing us to embrace our imperfections with greater ease. Focusing on gratitude can also help shift our perspective from what we lack to what we have. By appreciating our strengths and accomplishments, we can develop a more balanced and positive view of ourselves. Comparing ourselves to others is a surefire way to fuel perfectionism. Instead, let go of comparisons and focus on your unique journey and progress. Celebrate your achievements, no matter how small, and recognize that everyone has their own path.

Accepting that setbacks and failures are natural parts of life equips us to face challenges and recover more effectively. Perfectionism, on the other hand, stifles creativity and limits our ability to take risks or explore new possibilities. By letting go of the need for perfection, we create space for innovative thinking and creative solutions, unlocking potential we might otherwise suppress.

Embracing imperfection not only fosters resilience but also paves the way for a more fulfilling and authentic life. By letting go of the relentless pursuit of perfection, we open ourselves to creativity, adaptability, and greater happiness. This mindset shift allows us to focus on growth and meaningful connections rather than unattainable ideals. As Marianne Williamson beautifully puts it, "We are not perfect, but we are whole." Accepting this truth frees us from the weight of unrealistic expectations, enabling us to grow, learn, and connect with others on a deeper, more genuine level.

This shift not only enhances our ability to adapt but also leads to greater happiness and well-being. When we stop chasing an unattainable ideal and embrace ourselves as we are, we free ourselves from unnecessary pressure, allowing more joy and contentment to flow into our lives. Embracing imperfection, then, is not just about resilience—it's about living more authentically and fully.

Embracing imperfection means accepting that failure and setbacks are part of the human experience. When we stop looking for an unattainable ideal and learn to accept ourselves as we are, we become more resilient and adaptable.

Resilience and Adaptability

Eckhart Tolle, a renowned spiritual teacher, highlights the significance of living in the present moment and accepting things as they are in his book *The Power of Now*. He writes, "Whatever the present moment contains, accept it as if you had chosen it. Always work with it, not against it." This perspective encourages us to embrace imperfections and challenges as they arise, fostering resilience and adaptability.

Wim Hof, known as the "Iceman" for his extraordinary ability to withstand extreme cold, advocates for embracing discomfort as a path to resilience. Hof's method, which includes breathing exercises and cold exposure, teaches individuals to adapt to stress and build mental and physical resilience. Hof often says, "The cold is merciless but righteous. It reveals the true nature of your mental power." By willingly facing discomfort, we learn to adapt and strengthen.

In *Feel the Fear and Do It Anyway*, Susan Jeffers explores how confronting our fears and embracing discomfort can lead to greater resilience. She writes, "We cannot escape fear. We can only transform it into a companion that accompanies us on all our exciting adventures." This perspective reinforces the idea that embracing imperfection and discomfort can be instrumental in building mental strength.

Resilience is closely linked to the concept of "grit," a term popularized by psychologist Angela Duckworth. In her book *Grit: The Power of Passion and Perseverance*, Duckworth defines grit as the combination of passion and perseverance toward long-term goals. She asserts that talent alone is insufficient for success; sustained effort and resilience are essential. Duckworth writes, "Grit is living life like it's a marathon, not a sprint." This mindset encourages us to persist through challenges, recognizing that resilience is cultivated through consistent effort over time.

Serena Williams, one of the greatest tennis players of all time, has faced numerous setbacks and challenges throughout her career, including injuries and personal struggles such as postpartum depression. Despite challenges, she has consistently demonstrated resilience and adaptability, returning to the sport with renewed determination. After giving birth, Williams struggled with severe health complications but made a remarkable comeback to professional tennis. She has said, "I really think a champion is defined not by their wins but by how they can recover when they fall."

In the business world, resilience and adaptability are essential for success. Steve Jobs, faced significant failures, including being ousted from the company he helped create. However, he used these setbacks as opportunities for growth and innovation. After leaving Apple, Jobs founded NeXT, which eventually led to his return to Apple. He transformed the company with groundbreaking products like the iMac, iPod, and iPhone. Jobs once said, "I'm convinced that about half of what separates the successful entrepreneurs from the non-successful ones is pure perseverance."

Barack Obama, the 44th President of the United States, faced numerous challenges during his presidency, from the 2008 financial crisis to intense political opposition, particularly from a divided Congress. His ability to adapt to changing circumstances and maintain resilience was evident in his leadership. For example, his administration's response to the financial crisis involved adapting strategies and policies to stabilize the economy and support recovery. Obama has said, "The real test is not whether you avoid this failure because you won't. It's whether you let it harden or shame you into inaction, or whether you learn from it; whether you choose to persevere."

The Sacred Sons, a movement dedicated to men's work

and spiritual growth, highlights resilience and adaptability as essential qualities for personal transformation. Their teachings emphasize embracing vulnerability and imperfection, recognizing these as powerful pathways to inner strength and growth. Through practices such as breathwork, intentional movement, and emotional expression, the Sacred Sons provide men with tools to cultivate these traits. Their retreats and workshops create a supportive, brotherhood-oriented space where men can explore their vulnerabilities, foster connection, and collectively build resilience.

Embracing a growth mindset allows us to accept imperfections and setbacks as integral parts of the learning process, ultimately fostering resilience and adaptability.

In addition to mindset, emotional intelligence is another key factor in resilience and adaptability. Daniel Goleman, a psychologist and author of *Emotional Intelligence*, emphasizes the importance of being aware of and managing our emotions. Emotional intelligence (EQ) involves recognizing our emotional responses to challenges and using that awareness to adapt and respond effectively. Goleman writes, "What really matters for success, character, happiness, and lifelong achievements is a definite set of emotional skills—your EQ—not just purely cognitive abilities that are measured by conventional IQ tests."

In addition to emotional intelligence and social support, physical well-being is essential for resilience and adaptability. Maintaining a healthy lifestyle through regular exercise, proper nutrition, and adequate sleep enhances both physical and mental resilience. Exercise, in particular, has been shown to reduce stress and improve mood, facilitating better coping strategies for challenges. A systematic review and analysis published in *The BMJ* in 2024 found that various forms of exercise, including walking, jogging, yoga, and resistance training, were associated with reductions in depressive symptoms, with effects comparable to those of psychotherapy and pharmacotherapy.

This underscores the critical role exercise plays in promoting emotional well-being and fostering overall psychological resilience. Perhaps, then, we can view exercise as a healthier alternative to coping agents like alcohol, sugar and bingeing Netflix—offering not just temporary distraction, but lasting benefits for both body and mind. As we discussed earlier, the key is to take action. Simply thinking about going to the gym or planning an elaborate routine isn't enough—it's the act of starting, no matter how small, that drives real change. Whether it's a five-minute walk or a single yoga pose, every step forward matters. Taking those steps becomes even more powerful when paired with strong social connections. Research shows that these relationships enhance our ability to cope with stress and recover from setbacks. Psychologist Susan Pinker, in her book *The Village Effect*, explores the profound impact of social ties on well-being and resilience. She notes, *'People who are more socially connected live longer, are healthier, and cope better with life's challenges.'* This aligns with earlier discussions about the importance of community, such as in the Blue Zones of Japan, where strong social bonds contribute to remarkable longevity and well-being.

Becoming more Resilient and Adaptable

Wim Hof's method, which includes breathing exercises and cold exposure, highlights the connection between physical well-being and resilience. By training our bodies to adapt to stress, we can build both physical and mental resilience. One of Hof's practices involves taking a 20-second cold shower every day for a week. This simple exercise can help improve circulation, boost the immune system, and increase mental toughness. Hof's practices demonstrate that resilience can be developed through physical challenges and that our bodies are capable of adapting to extreme conditions.

Another important aspect of resilience is the ability to find meaning and purpose in our experiences. Viktor Frankl, a Holocaust survivor and psychiatrist, explored this concept in his book *Man's Search for Meaning*. He wrote, *'When we are no longer able to change a situation, we are challenged to change ourselves.'* Discovering meaning in our experiences, even in the face of adversity, can significantly enhance resilience and help us adapt to difficult circumstances. Frankl found purpose by assisting fellow prisoners in finding meaning in their suffering, which, in turn, gave him the strength to endure the horrors of the concentration camps. His logotherapy, a form of existential analysis, underscores the importance of finding purpose as a cornerstone of mental and emotional well-being.

Similarly, cultivating gratitude can serve as a practical way to find meaning and ground ourselves in the present. By appreciating life's existing blessings, we often uncover a sense of purpose that might otherwise go unnoticed. Together, logotherapy and gratitude remind us that purpose isn't always found in grand achievements but often in the simple, everyday moments that bring fulfillment and connection. In fact, research shows that practicing gratitude can significantly enhance mental health, reduce stress, and improve overall well-being. By focusing on the positive aspects of life, gratitude fosters a more optimistic perspective, making it easier to cope with challenges. Robert Emmons, a leading researcher on gratitude, explains in his book *Thanks! How Practicing Gratitude Can Make You Happier* that gratitude shifts our mindset and builds resilience, allowing us to navigate difficulties with greater ease.

Practicing gratitude doesn't require grand gestures; it can involve simple daily habits, such as keeping a gratitude journal or expressing appreciation to others. Regularly reflecting on what we are thankful for helps build a positive outlook and strengthens our ability to handle adversity. For instance, a middle-aged man who loathes his corporate job and daily commute might find gratitude in his family's health, his supportive spouse, or the opportunity to provide for his loved ones. By focusing on these blessings, he can shift his perspective and discover meaning even in an otherwise frustrating situation. This shift in perspective connects directly to the broader qualities of resilience and adaptability—essential traits for navigating life's complexities. When we focus less on ourselves and more on our connections with others, we create a foundation for growth and recovery. By embracing imperfection and adopting a growth mindset, we develop the ability to bounce back from setbacks and adapt to new conditions. Resilience is not built in isolation; it thrives on self-awareness, self-compassion, and community.

Michael Jordan, widely regarded as one of the greatest basketball players of all time, faced numerous setbacks and failures, including being cut from his high school basketball team. However, his determination and adaptability led him to become an NBA legend. Jordan once reflected, "I've missed more than 9,000 shots in my career. I've lost almost 300 games. Twenty-six times, I've been trusted to take the game-winning shot and missed. I've failed over and over and over again in my life. And that is why I succeed." His resilience extended beyond basketball. Jordan's business acumen demonstrates adaptability in a different arena. The Jordan brand, a subsidiary of Nike, has become a best-seller and a significant revenue generator for the company. This shows that adaptability and resilience are not only vital on the court but also in navigating challenges and opportunities throughout life.

In business, resilience and adaptability are essential for navigating the ever-changing landscape. Amazon founder, Jeff Bezos, is known for his ability to adapt and innovate in response to challenges. Bezos once said, "What's dangerous is not to evolve." His willingness to take risks and learn from failures has been a driving force behind Amazon's success. Amazon's transformation from an online bookstore to a global e-commerce giant involved numerous risks and innovations, such as the introduction of Amazon Prime and the development of Amazon Web Services (AWS).

Similarly, Elon Musk, CEO of Tesla and SpaceX, has demonstrated remarkable resilience and adaptability in his entrepreneurial ventures. Musk has faced numerous setbacks, including failed rocket launches and production challenges. However, his persistence and ability to adapt have led to groundbreaking achievements in both the automotive and aerospace industries. Musk's approach to failure is captured in his quote, "Failure is an option here. If things are not failing, you are not innovating enough." Musk's ability to handle multiple critical problems simultaneously has been highlighted by those who work closely with him. His ex-wife, Talulah Riley, has remarked on his unique capacity to manage a constant influx of challenges, contributing to his success.

In the political arena, Nelson Mandela, former President of South Africa, is a powerful example of resilience. Mandela endured 27 years of imprisonment for his anti-apartheid activism but emerged with a vision of reconciliation and unity for his country. Mandela's resilience and adaptability were evident in his ability to forgive and work with his former oppressors to build a new South Africa. He once said, "Do not judge me by my successes, judge me by how many times I fell down and got back up again."

Jon Kabat-Zinn, a pioneer in the field of consciousness, writes in his book *Wherever You Go, There You Are*, "You can't stop the waves, but you can learn to surf." This metaphor beautifully encapsulates the essence of resilience and adaptability—while we cannot control all the challenges that come our way, we can learn to navigate them with skill and presence.

Meditation teacher Sharon Salzberg also highlights the connection between consciousness and resilience in her book *Real Happiness*. She explains that mindfulness enables us to observe our thoughts and emotions without judgment, fostering greater emotional resilience. By cultivating mindfulness, we can respond to challenges with clarity and calmness instead of succumbing to stress and reactivity.

Another important aspect of resilience is the ability to set and maintain healthy boundaries. Nedra Glover Tawwab, therapist and author of *Set Boundaries, Find Peace*, emphasizes that boundaries are essential for protecting our mental and emotional well-being. She writes, "Boundaries are the gateway to healthy relationships." By defining what we are willing to accept in our interactions, boundaries safeguard our energy and create space for resilience and adaptability. Setting boundaries at work might involve limiting after-hours communication to preserve a healthy work-life balance or restricting interactions with a challenging colleague by keeping discussions strictly professional.

Just as boundaries protect our external energy, the practice of self-compassion nurtures our internal resilience. Kristin Neff's research on self-compassion highlights the importance of treating ourselves with kindness and understanding, particularly during difficult times. She writes, "Self-compassion provides an island of calm, a refuge from the stormy seas of endless positive and negative self-judgment." By fostering a supportive inner dialogue, self-compassion complements the external stability that boundaries provide, together creating a foundation for greater resilience and adaptability.

By celebrating the beauty of imperfection and fostering a culture of acceptance and support, we can aim to create a world where resilience and adaptability become collective strengths rather than solely individual traits. This shared commitment to growth and understanding can help us navigate challenges together, transforming our imperfections into opportunities for connection and progress.

Perhaps that, ultimately, is the goal—to thrive not just as individuals, but as a community bound by empathy, compassion, and the shared belief in our potential to grow. Let us embrace our wholeness, connection with others and find beauty in all our imperfections.

CHAPTER 13

THE WAY OUT OF...SELF

As we journey through life, many of us are drawn to self-help as a way to navigate challenges, achieve our goals, and find personal fulfillment. It's natural to want to improve ourselves— to become better, happier, and more successful. However, in this pursuit of self-improvement, it's easy to become overly focused on our own growth, to the point where we lose sight of the bigger picture.

Self-help promises solutions to our problems, but it can also perpetuate them. The more we strive to fix ourselves, the more we may come to see ourselves as broken or inadequate. The more we chase after happiness, the more elusive it can become. This is because self-help often focuses on what's wrong with us—what needs to be improved, changed, or fixed—rather than encouraging us to accept and embrace ourselves as we are.

What if a better approach to living involves focusing less on fixing ourselves and more on embracing those imperfections, fostering stronger connections, and addressing the broader realities of life? Is self-help genuinely beneficial, or does it risk trapping us in a cycle of endless self-obsession?

At some point, we may have to arrive at a profound realization that we are often the source of our own problems. This insight can be both enlightening and transformative. By acknowledging that our thoughts, behaviors, and beliefs contribute to the challenges we face, we empower ourselves to initiate meaningful change.

So, what's the solution? How do we navigate the world of self-help without burning out or losing ourselves in the process? Should we just stop trying to improve ourselves? Maybe...

The key is to recognize that self-improvement is just one aspect of a fulfilling life—not the only one. Focus on one or two areas at a time, and give yourself permission to rest and recharge along the way. Remember, growth is a gradual process, not a race, and it certainly doesn't have a finish line. It's easy to get caught up in the idea that we need to be constantly improving, but it's important to set realistic expectations for ourselves. Understand that there will be ups and downs, and that it's okay to have setbacks. Progress isn't always linear, and it's important to celebrate the small wins along the way.

One of the most liberating realizations on the self-help journey is that it's okay to be imperfect. Being human means having flaws, and that's not something to fix but to embrace. Growth doesn't require constant self-criticism; it calls for self-compassion—a shift in mindset that allows us to see imperfections as part of our unique humanity.

In the self-help world, it's easy to become consumed by the pursuit of external goals: achieving more, being more successful, or meeting societal standards of appearance. But at the end of the day, true fulfillment lies in peace of mind, which is often reflected in the quality of our relationships. Are we showing kindness, helping others, and engaging meaningfully with those around us? Or are we stuck in our own heads, isolating, or avoiding difficult interactions?

Equally important is asking whether we are trying to change others before looking inward at ourselves. True personal growth happens when we focus on connection, humility, and accountability—engaging with people, including those we may have conflicts with, and learning to value relationships over perfection. Peace of mind doesn't come from fixing everything about ourselves or others; it's found in acceptance, connection, and the shared humanity that gives life its meaning.

Above all, make sure that your self-improvement efforts are aligned with your core values and that they enhance your life, rather than detract from it.

In the rush to improve, we often forget to pause and reflect on how far we've come. Taking time to reflect on your journey can help you gain perspective and appreciate the progress you've made. It can also help you identify areas where you may need to adjust your approach or take a step back.

Take it Easy

Sometimes, you can do too much self-helping. There's always something more to do, another book to read, another strategy to try. This relentless pursuit can make it difficult to ever feel truly satisfied or content with where you are. And self-help could be seen as an addiction or a problem if done in isolation from the rest of your life.

You might find yourself constantly evaluating your progress, comparing yourself to others, and feeling like you're never quite good enough. This can lead to a sense of inadequacy, even as you make strides in your personal development. One of the reasons self-help can be so exhausting is that it often sets up unrealistic expectations. We're bombarded with messages that tell us we can have it all—perfect health, financial success, fulfilling relationships, and inner peace—if we just follow the right steps. But life is complex, and the reality is that we can't always control the outcomes. Sometimes, despite our best efforts, things don't go according to plan. Yet, the self-help industry often implies that if we're not succeeding, it's because we're not trying hard enough, not thinking positively enough, or not following the right advice. This can create a cycle of guilt and frustration, where we push ourselves even harder, only to feel more exhausted and less fulfilled.

One of the core arguments of the anti-self-help movement is its critique of individualism. Many self-help teachings emphasize personal success, self-reliance, and self-optimization, often at the expense of community, relationships, and social responsibility. Sceptics argue that this focus on the individual can lead to isolation and a lack of connection with others. By promoting the idea that everyone is responsible for their own success or failure, self-help can inadvertently foster a sense of competition and self-interest rather than cooperation and mutual support.

Ultimately, perhaps true fulfillment doesn't come from perpetually striving to improve ourselves but from finding peace with who we are, building meaningful connections with others, and trusting in something outside of ourselves. By embracing this mix, we can shift the focus from perfection to purpose, from isolation to community, and from self-centeredness to collective well-being.

Spiritual Solution

Many argue that true liberation from the confines of the self comes not through relentless self-improvement, but through humility, surrender, and a sense of belonging to a larger whole. This could be framed as spirituality, a higher purpose, or simply an acknowledgment of our interconnectedness with the world. Such perspectives offer an alternative path—one that emphasizes meaning, connection, and purpose beyond the self.

This "something greater" can be broadly defined as anything outside of oneself—outside the confines of our own minds. It could be an energy source, the universe, the natural world, or even the simple act of letting go and trusting in forces beyond our control. Just as we cannot hear certain frequencies like a dog whistle, who's to say we can fully comprehend or perceive the vastness of existence? Regardless of how it is defined, this concept invites us to expand our focus, shifting from a self-centered narrative to one that embraces interconnectedness and awe for the unknown.

By introducing this broader perspective, we challenge the self-help industry's fixation on personal mastery and self-reliance. Instead of centering solely on individual effort, we are reminded of our place within a larger, often incomprehensible, order. This perspective fosters humility, encourages collaboration, and cultivates a sense of wonder in the face of life's mysteries.

Ultimately, acknowledging something greater allows us to move beyond the limits of traditional self-help. It reframes the journey toward purpose and meaning as one of trust, acceptance, and connection—an approach that goes beyond self and embraces the richness of the world around us.

For God's Sake

For many, spiritual practice provides an alternative to the self-help approach of books and online courses. Rather than focusing on self-improvement and personal success, spirituality emphasizes connection, purpose, and surrender to a force outside of ourselves. Practices such as prayer, meditation, and communal gathering provide a sense of grounding and peace that can be difficult to achieve through a self-help book alone.

Different spiritual practices can offer guidance and support that goes beyond the individual, fostering a sense of belonging and purpose that exceeds the self.

> **Christianity:** Emphasizes a personal relationship with God, viewing the self as a creation of God, inherently sinful but redeemable through divine grace. Personal growth involves aligning oneself with God's will, seeking salvation, and embodying Christ-like virtues.

> **Buddhism:** Rejects the notion of a permanent self and does not assert a creator god. The focus is on realizing the impermanent and interdependent nature of life, leading to enlightenment. Self-improvement is pursued through ethical living, meditation, and wisdom to rise above suffering.

> **Hinduism:** Recognizes the self as inherently divine and at one with an ultimate reality. Personal development involves realizing this unity through various paths like devotion, knowledge, and disciplined practice.

Islam: Stresses the submission of the self to God. Humans are viewed as servants of God, and personal growth is achieved by following divine guidance.

Judaism: The self is viewed as a partner with God in the ongoing process of creation and repair of the world, highlighting a collaborative relationship rather than one of submission.

These differing views shape cultural approaches to self-improvement, whether through reliance on divine guidance or the pursuit of inner wisdom.

Interestingly, even among agnostics or those who reject traditional notions of the divine, expressions of faith often emerge in critical moments. Instinctive reactions—such as praying during a turbulent flight or uttering religious shrieks in moments of anger or desperation—reveal a human tendency to reach for something greater in times of uncertainty or fear. This phenomenon, sometimes referred to as "symbolic religiosity," involves religious behavior detached from comprehensive observance or affiliation.

While secularism emphasizes control and the comforts of science, challenging times can prompt individuals to instinctively seek a semblance of a higher power, often without conscious awareness. This suggests that the inclination toward faith may be an inherent aspect of the human experience, manifesting even in those who identify as non-religious.

Throughout history, religious and spiritual leaders have

weighed in on the self-help debate, often offering perspectives that challenge the industry's focus on the self. The Dalai Lama, the spiritual leader of Tibetan Buddhism, emphasizes the importance of compassion, interconnectedness, and the pursuit of inner peace over material success. His teachings encourage individuals to look beyond themselves and to consider the well-being of others as central to their own happiness. This perspective counters the self-help industry's emphasis on personal achievement by suggesting that true fulfillment comes from living in harmony with the universe's will, not our own.

A significant tension in self-help and religious movements is balancing self-reliance with reliance on the Spirit. Self-help often encourages individuals to take control of their lives, set goals, and achieve personal success. However, this emphasis on self-reliance can sometimes conflict with the idea of trusting in a higher power and accepting that not everything is within our control.

Does true fulfillment come from within, or does it require a connection to something greater than oneself?

Who am I?

As we've learned, the journey of self-help is often marketed as a quick fix, a straightforward path to becoming a better version of ourselves. We're told that with the right mindset, habits, and tools, we can achieve personal transformation and, ultimately, happiness.

However, this promise of self-improvement can sometimes be misleading. Rather than offering a clear path to fulfillment, it can lead us into an endless cycle of striving, where the more we chase after an idealized version of ourselves, the more distant it seems to become. This paradox lies at the heart of self-help: in the pursuit of a "better self," we risk losing touch with who we truly are.

But there's a deeper truth to be found in the old adage, "To thine own self be true." Knowing yourself—truly understanding your needs, boundaries, and how to protect them—can be the key to genuine healing and growth. When you are in tune with who you are, you're better equipped to face external challenges, whether it's dealing with the loss of a loved one, a job, or navigating conflicts in your relationships.

This self-knowledge is not about endlessly seeking improvement but rather about grounding yourself in an understanding of what truly matters to you. By knowing yourself, you build a strong foundation that can help you handle whatever life throws your way, with resilience and clarity. This approach shifts the focus from a never-ending pursuit of perfection to a more centered and empowered way of living, where true contentment is not elusive but grounded in self-awareness and authenticity.

It's a Lifelong Practice

When we think about self-help, the idea of a marathon often comes to mind—a long, arduous journey that requires endurance, dedication, and significant effort. Yet, even a marathon has a finish line, a point where the runner can finally rest and celebrate their achievement. In contrast, the reality of the self-help journey resembles an ultra-marathon—a race that stretches on indefinitely, with no clear end in sight, continuing only until our last breath. This is no sprint; it captures the essence of embarking on a path of self-improvement: once you start, it becomes a lifelong pursuit, with new goals and challenges constantly emerging on the horizon. Once the genie is out of the bottle, there's no going back—you will be forever reflecting and striving to improve yourself.

Initially, you may feel energized and motivated, excited about the possibilities that lie ahead. You set goals, adopt new habits, and immerse yourself in the work of becoming a better person. But as you progress, you might realize that for every accomplishment, a new area requires attention. You lose weight, but now you need to build muscle. You stop drinking, but you seek another outlet to cope with life's stresses. The finish line keeps moving further away, and what once felt like progress can start to feel like an endless project.

On a self-help journey, there are moments when you might feel exhausted from the constant push and reflection, questioning whether it's all worth it. The pursuit of self-improvement can become all-consuming, leaving little room for rest, relaxation, or simply enjoying life as it is.

Sometimes, the path will be steep and challenging, and other times it will be smooth and easy. There will be moments of exhaustion, but also moments of joy and fulfillment. And just like in an ultra marathon, there will be times when you need to slow down, take a break, and enjoy the view. In this way, the ultra marathon of self-help becomes less about reaching a distant finish line and more about the experiences and growth that happen along the way. It's about learning to be present in the moment, appreciating the progress you've made, and recognizing that the journey itself is valuable—because nothing really exists other than the here and now. Remember that the ultimate goal is not perfection, but growth.

By embracing the journey with all its challenges and rewards, we can find fulfillment not in reaching some idealized version of ourselves, but in the process of revealing who we are meant to be. And in doing so, we can shift our focus from constantly striving to simply being—being present, being authentic, and being true to ourselves.

The Power of Connection

Having support can make all the difference. Surround yourself with people who encourage and uplift you, and don't be afraid to ask for help when you need it, which can be so hard to do, especially for men. Whether it's a friend, a mentor, or a therapist, having someone to talk to can help you stay grounded and keep things in perspective. We tend to overthink things, and hearing and sharing with others can really help us.

The power of connection within the context of community is as old as humanity itself. For centuries, people have lived in close-knit groups, relying on each other for support, protection, and companionship. In these communities, the well-being of the individual was closely tied to the well-being of the group. Personal success was not measured in isolation but was seen in the context of how one contributed to the greater good. This sense of interconnectedness is something that many of us have lost in modern society, where individualism often takes precedence over community. And this is why we are focused on the self in pretty much everything we do. This focus may lead us to become selfish, self-absorbed, and self-seeking.

Research consistently shows that strong social connections are one of the most significant predictors of happiness and well-being. People who are connected to others—whether through family, friendships, or community involvement—tend to live longer, healthier, and more fulfilling lives. These connections provide emotional support, reduce stress, and give us a sense of purpose. Focusing solely on self-improvement can sometimes lead to loneliness and disconnection. When we become too absorbed in our own goals and challenges, we may neglect our relationships or fail to engage with our communities. This isolation can undermine our efforts to improve ourselves, as it deprives us of the social support and sense of belonging that are essential for well-being.

To avoid this pitfall, it's important to balance personal development with a commitment to others, to service. This means recognizing that our growth is not just about achieving personal goals but also about how we contribute to the lives of those around us. By investing in our relationships and communities, we can enhance our own well-being while also making a positive impact on the world.

One of the most rewarding aspects of life is the opportunity to contribute to something larger than ourselves. Whether it's through volunteering, mentoring, or simply being a good friend or neighbor, these acts of service can bring a profound sense of fulfillment. When we help others, we not only make their lives better, but we also enrich our own. This is because giving to others taps into a fundamental aspect of human nature. We are wired to care for and connect with others, and when we act on this impulse, we experience a sense of joy and satisfaction that is difficult to achieve through self-centered pursuits. Numerous studies have shown that people who engage in acts of kindness and generosity report higher levels of happiness and life satisfaction than those who focus solely on their own needs.

Research from the University of British Columbia found that people who spent money on others reported greater happiness than those who spent it on themselves. Similarly, studies from the Greater Good Science Center at UC Berkeley have highlighted how acts of altruism and generosity lead to increased well-being and a sense of fulfillment. These findings are a testament to the power of giving and how it enriches our lives in ways that self-focused pursuits cannot. Contributing to the greater good can provide us with a sense of purpose that goes beyond our personal goals. It reminds us that we are part of something larger than ourselves—that our lives have meaning not just because of what we achieve, but because of the positive impact we have on others. This sense of purpose can be a powerful motivator, helping us to stay resilient in the face of challenges and to find meaning in our lives, even when things don't go as planned.

The pursuit of self-improvement can sometimes feel hollow if it's disconnected from a larger purpose. When we focus only on ourselves, we may achieve our goals, but we may also find that the satisfaction we feel is fleeting. True fulfillment comes from knowing that we are making a difference—that our lives have value not just because of what we gain, but because of what we give. While self-help often emphasizes the importance of self-reliance and individual effort, it's crucial to recognize that our personal growth is deeply influenced by our relationships. The people we surround ourselves with play a crucial role in shaping who we are and how we see the world. They provide us with support, challenge us to grow, and offer us different perspectives that can help us see things in new ways. A friend or partner who truly knows and understands us can help us see our strengths and potential when we are feeling down. They can offer encouragement and support when we are facing challenges, and they can help us stay grounded when we are feeling overwhelmed. Similarly, a mentor or teacher can provide guidance and wisdom that helps us navigate our personal and professional growth.

In this way, relationships are not just a source of emotional support—they are also a key factor in our personal development. By investing in our relationships, we can create a network of support that helps us achieve our goals and grow in meaningful ways.

Relationships provide us with opportunities to practice the skills and qualities that we are trying to develop. If we are working on becoming more patient, compassionate, or understanding, our relationships give us the chance to put these qualities into action. In this way, personal growth is not something that happens in isolation—it happens in the context of our interactions with others.

Another important aspect of balancing self-improvement with collective well-being is to be mindful of how our actions and choices affect others. This means being aware of how our pursuit of personal goals might impact our relationships or our community, and making adjustments as needed to ensure that we are not inadvertently causing harm. It also means being open to feedback from others and being willing to make changes if our actions are not aligned with our values or the needs of those around us.

CHAPTER 14

THE SOLUTION

As highlighted in previous chapters, true peace does not come from changing ourselves, but from letting go of the self (or ego) and its relentless drive to become "better." This process involves releasing the need for external validation and comparison, embracing self-acceptance, and recognizing that we are not in control.

The real "way out" isn't found in more self-focus but in releasing it entirely. When we shift our attention outward—toward others, toward connection, toward something greater—we rise above the limits of the self and discover a deeper sense of purpose and meaning. So, as a final step, simply try letting go.

Let go of the drive for perfection, the need to control, and the constant self-evaluation. Instead, embrace presence, openness, and the freedom that comes with simply being. Ironically, true growth often begins when we stop trying so hard to grow.

The ultimate goal of self-improvement is not to become a perfect version of ourselves, but to become a person who is compassionate, connected, and committed to making a positive difference in the world. By shifting our focus from self-centered growth to community-centered well-being, we can create a more balanced, fulfilling, and meaningful life for ourselves and those around us. True liberation from suffering arises when we diminish our focus on "me" and "self."

At the same time, it's important to recognize that we cannot give to others if we are not taking care of ourselves. We must put on our own oxygen mask first. Self-care is not selfish—it is essential for our well-being and our ability to contribute to others. By caring for our physical, emotional, and mental health, we ensure that we have the energy and resilience to support those around us. We must love ourselves first before we can fully receive or love others.

Self-care is about nurturing yourself in ways that replenish your energy and well-being, enabling you to show up fully for others. It's about setting boundaries, saying no when necessary, and ensuring that you aren't depleting your resources while giving. When we care for ourselves, we are better equipped to care for others, creating a positive cycle where our well-being fuels our ability to contribute meaningfully to the lives of those around us.

In this way, self-care and service are not mutually exclusive—they are deeply interconnected. By taking care of ourselves, we create a foundation from which we can give to others. And by giving to others, we reinforce our own sense of purpose and fulfillment, creating a life that is rich in both personal and collective well-being.

When we shift our focus from self-centered self-improvement to a more community-oriented approach, we open ourselves up to a whole new level of fulfillment. By investing in our relationships and communities, we create a sense of connection and belonging that is deeply rewarding. We also find that our personal growth is enhanced when we are surrounded by others who support and encourage us.

Moreover, by contributing to the greater good, we create a sense of purpose and meaning that goes beyond our individual achievements. We realize that our lives have value not just because of what we accomplish, but because of the positive impact we have on others. This sense of purpose can be a powerful source of motivation and resilience, helping us navigate challenges and setbacks with greater ease.

I am the Problem

When we reflect on the nature of problems, an interesting idea emerges: all problems are created by those who suffer them. This philosophical insight suggests that our perception of problems is shaped more by our internal world—our thoughts, beliefs, and attitudes—than by external circumstances. In essence, I am the problem; the self is often the issue. Understanding this can open the door to transforming how we approach and resolve the difficulties in our lives.

The idea that "all problems are created by those who suffer them" can be traced back to various philosophical and spiritual traditions. In Buddhism, for example, the concept of *dukkha* (often translated as "suffering" or "unsatisfactoriness") is central. It teaches that suffering arises not from external events, but from our attachments, desires, and aversions—our mental responses to those events. Similarly, Stoic philosophy emphasizes that it is not events themselves that disturb us, but our judgments about them. Marcus Aurelius, the Stoic philosopher and Roman emperor, wrote, "The soul becomes dyed with the color of its thoughts." This suggests that our experience of life, including our problems, is deeply influenced by how we think about and interpret the world around us.

Consider a simple everyday scenario: You are stuck in traffic, late for an important meeting or appointment. The situation itself—being in traffic—might seem like the problem. But if you dig deeper, you'll see that the real issue lies in your reaction to it. Your anxiety, frustration, or fear of being judged for being late are the actual sources of your suffering. Someone else in the same situation might use the time to listen to music or a podcast, experiencing no real distress at all. The problem, in this case, is not the traffic but how you perceive and respond to it. Your reaction.

Our perception of problems is often shaped by our mental and emotional frameworks. When we encounter a challenge, our minds immediately begin to interpret it, often magnifying the issue based on our fears, insecurities, and past experiences. This magnification can make problems seem more significant and impassable than they truly are. Imagine you receive critical feedback at work. If you struggle with self-esteem, your mind might interpret this feedback as a reflection of your worth, blowing it out of proportion. You might think, "I'm not good enough," or "I'm going to lose my job," even if the feedback is constructive and meant to help you improve. The problem isn't just the feedback; it's your interpretation of it—how your mind has framed the situation.

Self-help practices can sometimes exacerbate this magnification. When self-help focuses too much on identifying and fixing flaws, it can lead to an obsession with perceived shortcomings.

You begin to see problems everywhere—in your habits, thoughts, and relationships—because you're constantly searching for what's wrong and how to improve it. This relentless focus on problems can create a cycle where minor issues are blown out of proportion, making life feel like a series of crises to manage.

I am the Solution

However, when we recognize that our perception plays a central role in creating problems, we gain the power to change how we experience them. The first step is awareness—becoming conscious of how we're interpreting situations and how those interpretations are contributing to our suffering. Once we're aware, we can begin to question our automatic thoughts and challenge the narratives we've created around our problems.

One of the most effective ways to transform how we experience problems is by shifting our focus. This could mean redirecting our attention from ourselves to others, or from dwelling on the past or future to being fully present in the moment. When we make this shift, the weight of our problems often feels lighter, and in some cases, the problems themselves seem to fade. By stepping out of self-centered or time-bound thinking, we gain a broader perspective, allowing us to approach challenges with greater clarity and ease.

When we're consumed by a problem, our attention often turns inward. We focus on how the issue affects us—how it makes us feel, what it means for our future, or how others perceive us. This inward focus can magnify our suffering, trapping us in a cycle of self-preoccupation.

Consider someone grieving the loss of a loved one. The pain

and grief can feel all-encompassing, making it easy to become lost in those emotions. However, shifting focus outward— perhaps by offering support to other grieving family members or volunteering to help others facing similar losses—can alleviate the intensity of personal suffering. Engaging with others in meaningful ways creates a sense of purpose and connection, which can soften the edges of our own pain. In helping others, we often find healing for ourselves.

Many of our problems are tied to worries about the future or regrets about the past. We might be anxious about a work presentation next week, or we might ruminate on a mistake we made last month. These concerns, while valid, are often projections of our minds rather than reflections of current reality (and it's important to recognize that).

The practice of bringing our attention to the present offers a powerful moment of relief from this problem-focused mindset. When we focus on the here and now, we can reduce the mental noise that amplifies the committee in our heads. Instead of worrying about what might happen or dwelling on what has already passed, we concentrate on what is actually happening in the present moment. By focusing on the here and now, we can significantly reduce the future-oriented anxiety that magnifies the problem.

Another approach is to reframe problems not as obstacles, but as opportunities for growth and learning. This doesn't mean ignoring the difficulties we face, but rather viewing them through a different lens. When we see problems as challenges that can teach us something valuable, they become less about suffering and more about development, or growth.

Facing a difficult conversation with a colleague might initially feel like a problem. You might dread the potential conflict and stress about the possible outcomes. But if you reframe the situation as an opportunity to improve communication skills or to strengthen the relationship, the problem starts to transform. It becomes a chance to learn, to grow, and to become more resilient. This reframing aligns with the Stoic idea that obstacles can be turned to our advantage.

Marcus Aurelius famously wrote, "The impediment to action advances action. What stands in the way becomes the way." By embracing problems as part of our path, we can shift our focus from what's wrong to how we can engage with the situation positively.

Understanding that many of our problems are shaped by our perceptions doesn't mean that all difficulties are simply in our heads or that they're not real. Life presents genuine challenges that require attention and action. However, by recognizing the role our minds play in creating and magnifying problems, we empower ourselves to respond more effectively.

By shifting our focus—from self to others, from the future to the present, and from problems to opportunities—we can diminish the suffering associated with our challenges and perhaps even transform those challenges into meaningful experiences.

As you continue on your self-help journey, remember to look beyond yourself. Seek out opportunities to connect with others, contribute to a community, and make a difference in the lives of those around you. Remember that true fulfillment comes not just from what you achieve for yourself, but from the positive impact you have on the world around you.

Self-improvement is not just about becoming the best version of yourself—it's about becoming a person who is part of a larger whole, someone who contributes to the well-being of others and who finds joy in the connections they build along the way. By embracing this collective journey, you can find a deeper sense of purpose, fulfillment, and happiness than you ever could on your own.

This inward focus is deeply ingrained in modern society. We're taught to measure success by individual achievements— our careers, our finances, and our physical appearance. However, we are inherently social creatures—human beings thrive on relationships, on the sense of belonging that comes from being part of a community. When we turn our attention away from ourselves and toward others, we can find a deeper sense of purpose and satisfaction.

So, as you move forward, make a commitment to balance your personal growth with a focus on community and connection. Let your self-improvement journey be one that not only enhances your own life but also enriches the lives of those around you. In doing so, you will find that the rewards of this journey are far greater than anything you could achieve alone.

Less Self more Freedom

The essence of a fulfilling life lies not just in improving who we are, but in how we connect with others, contribute to the greater good, and truly understand ourselves—knowing what we need, setting boundaries, and nourishing our inner selves. This new perspective invites us to shift our focus from self-centered goals to a more expansive view that includes the well-being of those around us. It encourages us to see our growth as intertwined with the growth of others and to recognize that our greatest strengths are often revealed in our relationships, communities, and collective efforts.

Start applying these insights in small, meaningful ways. Look for opportunities to connect with others, whether it's through lending a helping hand, sharing your time and skills, or simply being present and attentive to the needs of those around you. Remember that every positive interaction, no matter how small, has the potential to create a ripple effect, fostering connection and strengthening the bonds that hold us together. Embrace the idea that your growth is not solely about becoming the best version of yourself, but also about making a positive impact on the lives of others.

Let your growth be more than just a personal journey— let it be a gift that enriches both your life and the lives of those around you.

Embracing a Freedom Beyond Self-Help

This book is for those of you standing at the crossroads, unsure of where to turn, and perhaps just beginning to consider that there might be a different way to live. It's not for the seasoned self-helper or wellness enthusiast who may already have all the answers—it's for the beginner, the one starting to realize that the solutions they've been seeking might not come from the latest guru fad or quick-fix trend. And that the solution to our struggles are not found in a constant push to "improve" ourselves, but in accepting ourselves fully, as we are, in this very moment.

What you've read here is just the beginning. These insights mark the start of a lifetime of practices and realizations that will guide you toward greater self-awareness, freedom, and peace. It's a journey not about doing more, but about being more—living more consciously, with intention. It's about understanding that we're not in control of how everything unfolds and that, often, the best course of action is to simply surrender to the flow of life.

If you've read this far, you've already taken the first step toward a new perspective—a shift that can open up new possibilities for growth, connection, and purpose. And that's where the real journey begins. So, don't wait for a perfect moment, a perfect plan, or a perfect version of yourself. The freedom you seek is already here, waiting for you to notice. Let go of the constant need to improve, embrace life's imperfections, and start living now. Recognize that you are enough, just as you are, and that by stepping away from the fixation on self, you'll discover a world of connection, peace, and meaning that has always been available to you. Now take that next step.

CHAPTER 15
OVER TO YOU

I want to leave you with one final reflection and a summary of what is laid out in this book. Life is messy, complicated, and often resistant to neat solutions. And yet, we continue searching for those elusive answers, oscillating between aspirations and setbacks, trying to piece together a self that feels whole. Regardless of the route we choose, we all share a common goal— to move from what we think or feel is broken toward what we believe will make us happy.

We have a universal yearning to reconcile the disjointed parts of ourselves, whether we live in small-town America or bustling cities in Asia. We all seek coherence amid chaos, clarity amid confusion. But here's the twist: what if the self isn't a puzzle to be completed? What if our pieces were never meant to fit together neatly?

Throughout this book, we've explored the contradictions of self-help—the ways it promises freedom while often binding us tighter to self-obsession, and the industry's knack for turning profound questions into marketable soundbites. We've also examined alternatives: community, service, and surrender to something greater than ourselves. Now, as we reach the end, it's your turn to decide how to integrate these ideas into your life—or whether to discard them altogether.

You Are Not Broken

If there's one thing I hope you take away from these pages, it's this: being human means being a work in progress. Our uneven selves defy the linear trajectories sold to us by self-help books and productivity gurus. One moment we're climbing toward our goals with purpose and determination; the next, we're sliding backward into old habits and insecurities. This isn't failure—it's life.

When we stop demanding perfection, we create space for growth that is organic, not forced. Embracing imperfection doesn't mean giving up on self-improvement; it means letting go of the illusion that we can—or should—control every aspect of our journey. Instead of asking, "How can I fix myself?" we might ask, "How can I live more fully, here and now?"

Beyond the Self

In the Buddhist tradition, the concept of *Anatta*—or "no-self"—challenges the very premise of self-help. It suggests that the self we work so hard to improve is an illusion, a construct of shifting thoughts, emotions, and perceptions. Clinging to this illusion, Buddhism teaches, is the root of suffering. Liberation comes not from perfecting the self but from letting go of it entirely.

This idea may feel radical, even unsettling. After all, much of Western culture revolves around the idea of selfhood—defining it, asserting it, and enhancing it. But consider this:

some of the most meaningful experiences in life come when we lose ourselves. In the flow of creativity, the embrace of a loved one, or the quiet awe of nature, we glimpse a freedom far richer than any self-help program could offer.

Your Turn

As you close this book, consider where you are in your own journey. Are you striving to piece your life together, or are you ready to let it unfold as it will? Are you clinging to a vision of your ideal self, or are you willing to embrace the messy, imperfect reality of who you are right now?

Keep in mind that there is no one-size-fits-all answer. What works for me may not work for you, and that's okay. The beauty of life lies in its diversity and unpredictability. The path forward isn't a straight line; it's a winding road, full of detours, dead ends, and unexpected vistas.

So, over to you. However you choose to sit with your thoughts, know that there is no "wrong" way to be. Trust your instincts, be patient with yourself, and above all, remember that your worth isn't measured by your job, your social network, or your ability to follow a guru's ten-step plan.

The self-help industry may sell the promise of a better you, but the truth is, you're already enough: perfectly irregular, gloriously unfinished, and beautifully human.

"The one important thing I have learned over the years is the difference between taking one's work seriously and taking one's self seriously. The first is imperative and the second is disastrous".

Margot Fonteyn

PRACTICAL STEPS

How To Stop Thinking About *Your* Self

Here are some fresh, alternative takes on personal growth that ditch the traditional self-help remedies. These ideas are practical, everyday ways to step outside yourself and grow—no yoga studios, pricey subscription programs, or special training required. You can start right now and make it your own. Explore these approaches and see what clicks for you!

Exercise 1 : Get Over Yourself - Active Listening

Unlike traditional meditation, active listening doesn't require solitude or silence—it invites you to engage fully with another person. By focusing entirely on what someone else is saying, you naturally quiet your own inner dialogue and immerse yourself in the present moment. Think of it as mindfulness in motion. Here's how to practice active listening:

Find Your Space:

Choose an opportunity to engage in a meaningful conversation. It could be with a friend, colleague, or even a family member. Aim for a time and place where you can focus without distractions, such as during a quiet coffee chat or while on a walk.

Settle In:

Before you begin, take a moment to ground yourself. Take a few deep breaths to clear your mind and set the intention to be fully present for the conversation. Remind yourself that this is an opportunity to give your full attention to someone else.

Focus on the Speaker:

As the person speaks, direct your full attention to their words, tone, and body language. Resist the urge to interrupt or plan your response. Instead, focus entirely on understanding their perspective. Let their voice anchor you in the present.

Suspend Judgment:

Avoid forming opinions, solving problems, or analyzing what's being said. Instead, adopt a curious and open mindset. Remind yourself that your goal is to understand, not to agree or disagree.

Reflect Back:

Once the speaker pauses, summarize or reflect on what you heard to show you're engaged. For example, say, "It sounds like you're saying X," or, "I can hear how important this is to you." This not only validates their experience but also helps you confirm your understanding.

Embrace Silence:

Allow for natural pauses in the conversation. Resist the urge to fill every gap with words. Silence can create space for the speaker to share more deeply and for you to process what you've heard.

Practice Gratitude:

At the end of the conversation, express your gratitude for the opportunity to connect. A simple, "Thank you for sharing that with me," can go a long way in building trust and mutual respect.

Reflection Prompt

- How did it feel to focus entirely on the speaker without thinking about your own response?
- Did you notice moments when your mind wandered, and how did you bring your focus back?
- How did the speaker respond to being listened to fully?
- What did you learn about the speaker—and yourself— during this exercise?

Why This Matters

Active listening is a practice that moves past self-focus. It not only cultivates empathy and connection but also quiets your inner chatter, giving your mind a moment of rest. For the listener, it's an opportunity to step outside your own concerns and experience the world through someone else's perspective. For the speaker, the benefits are equally profound—they feel heard, valued, and understood. By practicing active listening, you strengthen relationships and foster trust, all while grounding yourself in the present moment. Try it out—it's a small shift that can have a profound impact on your day and your relationships.

Exercise 2: Discover Yourself – Book a Solo Trip Abroad

Traveling solo is one of the most eye-opening ways to step outside of yourself—literally and figuratively. When you're navigating unfamiliar places alone, there's no one to distract you or fill the silence. It's just you, your thoughts, and the world around you. The goal? To learn who you really are when you're out of your comfort zone and away from familiar distractions. Here's how to get started:

Pick a Destination That Unsettles You (no war zones):

Choose a place that feels just outside your comfort zone—not extreme, but challenging enough to stretch you. It could be a country where you don't speak the language, a bustling city full of energy, or even a remote mountain community. The key is to pick a destination that feels exciting and a little uneasy.

Plan the Essentials, But Stay Flexible:

Book your flights, find a safe and comfortable place to stay, and map out the basics for your first few days. But leave room for the unexpected—solo travel is as much about discovery as it is about preparation.

Embrace Being Alone:

Commit to spending intentional time on your own. Avoid packing your schedule too tightly. Instead, do things like sitting in an unfamiliar café and ordering something you've never tried, wander without Google Maps, or walk through a busy city for an hour with no plan. Let yourself feel the moments and immerse yourself in your surroundings.

Challenge Yourself to Engage:

Push yourself to connect with others, even if it feels awkward. Chat with locals or share a table with other travelers. These interactions can reveal a lot about how you relate to people in new and unfamiliar situations.

Notice Your Reactions:

Pay attention to your thinking during quiet moments and challenges. Are you uncomfortable being alone? Do you feel empowered by the independence? When frustrations arise— whether from a language barrier, getting lost, or dealing with loneliness—observe how you respond. These moments hold key insights into who you are and how you adapt.

Reflection Prompt

- How do you feel spending extended time alone—free, unsettled, or something in between?
- What patterns or thoughts are coming up when you're by yourself?
- How do you handle moments of discomfort, frustration, or even anger?
- What have you learned about yourself from being in this unfamiliar environment?

Why This Matters

The goal isn't to come home with all the answers or a life-changing epiphany. It's about learning through the experience— about yourself, your strengths, and how you face the world when it's just you and the unknown. Solo travel forces you to confront parts of yourself that might otherwise stay hidden. Embrace the journey and be open to whatever you find—you might just surprise yourself.

If a solo trip abroad feels out of reach, you can apply the same principles closer to home—like picking an unfamiliar city and being there alone. It's not about the scale of the adventure but about stepping into discomfort and observing yourself in that new environment.

Exercise 3: Let Go of Yourself - Write it Out

Holding a grudge is like drinking poison and hoping it harms someone else. They can keep us trapped in a cycle of anger and hurt. Writing them out is a simple yet powerful way to process these thoughts, understand their impact, and finally release them. Here's a straightforward guide to help you clear some emotional clutter:

Pinpoint the Grudge:

Start by identifying what's bugging you. Is it a person, a situation, or maybe even an institution? Be specific about what's causing that knot of irritation.

Write the Story:

Jot down exactly what happened. What did this person or situation do to spark those feelings? Be honest and detailed.

Check Your Role:

Take a minute to think about your part in this. Did you have unrealistic expectations? Contribute to the conflict? This isn't about taking the blame but about understanding your role in the bigger picture.

Consider the Cost:

How is holding onto this grudge affecting you? Is it eating away at your peace of mind? Straining your relationships? Notice the toll it's taking on your life.

Let It Go:

Once it's all written out, consciously release it. You can share it with someone you trust, burn it, or just make a personal commitment to move on. Whatever feels right for you.

Reflection Prompt

- How did it feel to write everything down?
- Did you learn something new about yourself or the situation?
- How might letting go of this grudge free up space for more positive energy in your life?

Why This Matters

This isn't about instant transformation—it's a process, and that's okay. Letting go of a grudge takes time and practice, but each time you release it, you're making room for more peace, clarity, and emotional freedom. You free up mental and emotional energy that was once tied up in anger, resentment, or hurt, allowing yourself to focus on what truly matters—your well-being, your growth, and the positive connections in your life. By letting go, you are choosing to prioritize your peace over holding onto negativity, and that shift, no matter how small, can create ripples of positive change throughout your life. Give it a shot and see what happens—you might be surprised at how much lighter and more present you feel once the clutter is cleared.

FURTHER READING

Here's a focused list that offers fresh insights and practical tools for personal growth, with yourself and others. Whether you're looking to shift a perspective, cultivate inner peace, or explore new ways to navigate the world, these titles are packed with inspiration and ideas that can actually make a difference. Take a look, and see which ones speak to where you are right now.

- "Leaving it All Behind" by Bhikkhuni Anandabodhi & Bhikkhuni Santacitta (2014)
- "The Four Noble Truths" by Venerable Ajahn Sumedho (2018)
- "Daring Greatly" by Brené Brown (2012)
- "The Architecture of Happiness" by Alain de Botton (2006)
- "A Return to Love" by Marianne Williamson (1992)
- "Iron John: A Book About Men" by Robert Bly (1990)
- "The Untethered Soul: The Journey Beyond Yourself" by Michael A. Singer (2007)
- "The Seven Spiritual Laws of Success" by Deepak Chopra (1994)
- "Feel the Fear and Do It Anyway" by Susan Jeffers (1987)
- "Sober Curious" by Ruby Warrington (2018)

- "The Power of Now: A Guide to Spiritual Enlightenment" by Eckhart Tolle (1997)
- "Man's Search for Meaning" by Viktor E. Frankl (1946)
- "Atomic Habits" by James Clear (2018)
- "The Subtle Art of Not Giving a Fuck" by Mark Manson (2016)
- "The Road Less Traveled" by M. Scott Peck (1978)
- "You Can Heal Your Life" by Louise Hay (1984)
- "Radical Acceptance" by Tara Brach (2003)
- "Think and Grow Rich" by Napoleon Hill (1937)
- "The 7 Habits of Highly Effective People" by Stephen R. Covey (1989)
- "Untamed" by Glennon Doyle (2020)
- "The Alchemist" by Paulo Coelho (1988)
- "The Artist's Way: A Spiritual Path to Higher Creativity" by Julia Cameron (1992)
- "The Miracle of Mindfulness" by Thich Nhat Hanh (1975)
- "Loving What Is: Four Questions That Can Change Your Life" by Byron Katie (2002)
- "Quiet" by Susan Cain (2012)
- "The War of Art" by Steven Pressfield (2002)
- "The Happiness Project" by Gretchen Rubin (2009)
- "How to Win Friends and Influence People" by Dale Carnegie (1936)
- "Self-Compassion: The Proven Power of Being Kind to Yourself" by Kristin Neff (2011)

ACKNOWLEDGEMENTS

I do want to express my gratitude to you, the reader, for taking the time to engage with this book. I hope it leaves you in a better place than it found you.

Connect with us at Selfish Books

Do you have a manifesto you're eager to share? Let us know.

selfishbooks@gmail.com
selfishbooks.com
@selfishbooksforyou